A PROPHETIC CALL TO IGNITE THE CHURCH

ABLAZE

A PROPHETIC CALL TO IGNITE THE CHURCH

Cindy Jacobs, Heidi Baker, Niko Njotorahardjo,
Rob Hoskins, Andy Byrd, and more

JERUSALEM 2020
EMPOWERED21 GLOBAL CONGRESS

Copyright © 2020 by Empowered21 Global Congress

Published by Four Rivers Media Group

All rights reserved. No portion of this book may be reproduced, stored in a retrieval system, or transmitted in any form or by any means—electronic, mechanical, photocopy, recording, scanning, or other—except for brief quotations in critical reviews or articles, without prior written permission of the author.

Scripture quotations marked KJV are taken from the King James Version of the Bible. Public domain. Scripture quotations marked NIV are taken from the Holy Bible, New International Version®, NIV®. Copyright © 1973, 1978, 1984, 2011 by Biblica, Inc.™ Used by permission of Zondervan. All rights reserved worldwide. www.zondervan.com. The "NIV" and "New International Version" are trademarks registered in the United States Patent and Trademark Office by Biblica, Inc.™ | Scripture quotations marked NKJV are taken from the New King James Version®. Copyright © 1982 by Thomas Nelson. Used by permission. All rights reserved. | Scripture quotations marked TLB are taken from The Living Bible copy- right © 1971 by Tyndale House Foundation. Used by permission of Tyndale House Publishers Inc., Carol Stream, Illinois 60188. All rights reserved. The Living Bible, TLB, and The Living Bible logo are registered trademarks of Tyndale House Publishers. | Scripture quotations marked NLT are taken from the *Holy Bible*, New Living Translation, copyright © 1996, 2004, 2015 by Tyndale House Foundation. Used by permission of Tyndale House Publishers, Inc., Carol Stream, Illinois 60188. All rights reserved. | Scripture quotations marked MSG are taken from THE MESSAGE, copyright © 1993, 1994, 1995, 1996, 2000, 2001, 2002 by Eugene H. Peterson. Used by permission of NavPress. All rights reserved. Represented by Tyndale House Publishers, Inc. | Scripture quotations marked GNT are from the Good News Translation in Today's English Version—Second Edition. Copyright © 1992 by American Bible Society. Used by Permission.

For foreign and subsidiary rights, contact the author.

ISBN: 9781950718351   1 2 3 4 5 6 7 8 9 10

Printed in the United States of America

JOIN BELIEVERS FROM

Around the World

JERUSALEM 2020
EMPOWERED21 GLOBAL CONGRESS

WHEN: May 31 - June 3, 2020   **LOCATION:** Pais Arena, Jerusalem

JERUSALEM 2020

EMPOWERED21 GLOBAL CONGRESS

BE A PART OF WHAT THE *Holy Spirit* IS DOING AROUND THE WORLD DURING PENTECOST 2020

YOU AND YOUR CHURCH ARE INVITED

Journey to Jerusalem May 31 - June 3, 2020 for a global gathering of Spirit-empowered believers from all over the world! Experience a once-in-a-lifetime opportunity to visit the Holy Land while uniting in prayer and worship, hearing from leading Spirit-led voices and discovering where the global church is headed in the future. Your life will never be the same as you encounter the Holy Spirit in a fresh and powerful way.

WHEN: May 31 - June 3, 2020
LOCATION: Pais Arena, Jerusalem

WORSHIP LED BY:
Planetshakers, Gateway Worship, Lindy Conant
AND OTHER GLOBAL ARTISTS!

EMPOWERED21 GLOBAL LEADERSHIP AND SPECIAL GUESTS INVITE YOU TO JERUSALEM2020

- E.A. Adeboye *(RCCG)*
- Michelle Bachmann *(USA)*
- Heidi Baker *(Iris Global)*
- Glyn Barrett *(Audacious Church)*
- Doug Beachem *(IPHC)*
- Lisa Bevere *(USA)*
- Charles Blake *(COGIC)*
- Reinhard Bonnke *(CfAN)*
- Jurgen Buhler *(ICEJ)*
- Glenn Burris *(Foursquare)*
- Dave Burrows *(BFM)*
- Andy Byrd *(YWAM)*
- Omar Cabrera *(Argentina)*
- Cesar Castellanos *(G12)*
- Juanita Cercone *(Enlace)*
- Hugo Chan *(Hong Kong)*
- Ishmael Charles *(COG)*
- Frank Chikane *(AFM)*
- Rick Ciaramitaro *(Canada)*

- Doug Clay *(AOG)*
- Samuel Clements *(COGOP)*
- Danny De Leon *(Templo Calvario)*
- Paul Dhinakaran *(Jesus Calls)*
- Chady El-Aouad *(ALC)*
- Russell Evans *(Planetshakers)*
- David Ferguson *(USA)*
- John Francis *(England)*
- Jentezen Franklin *(USA)*
- Claudio Freidzon *(Argentina)*
- Alton Garrison *(AOG)*
- Jonas Gonzalez *(Enlace)*
- Edward Grabovenko *(Russia)*
- Mart Green *(USA)*
- Bobby Gruenwald *(YouVersion)*
- Prince Guneratnam *(Malaysia)*
- Teo Hayashi *(Dunamis)*
- Arto Hamalainen *(PEM)*
- Fakhry Hanna *(Syria)*

- Tom Hess *(Israel)*
- Dag Heward-Mills *(Ghana)*
- Marilyn Hickey *(USA)*
- Timothy Hill *(COG)*
- Wayne Hilsden *(Israel)*
- Al Hollingsworth *(USA)*
- Rob Hoskins *(One Hope)*
- Brian Houston *(Hillsong)*
- Cindy Jacobs *(Generals Int.)*
- Bill Johnson *(Bethel)*
- Todd Johnson *(USA)*
- Shekhar Kallianpur *(India)*
- Scott Kelso *(USA)*
- Lawrence Khong *(Singapore)*
- Daniel Kolenda *(CFAN)*
- Michael Loulianos *(Jesus Image)*
- Young Hoon Lee *(Korea)*
- Dennis Lindsay *(CFNI)*
- Ron Luce *(USA)*

- Cash Luna *(Casa de Dios)*
- Henry Madava *(Ukraine)*
- Gordon McDonald *(PHCC)*
- Elvis Medina *(Domican Rep.)*
- Chadwick Mohan *(India)*
- Sam Monk *(Equippers)*
- Gordon Moore *(Australia)*
- Nathan Morris *(UK)*
- Robert Morris *(Gateway)*
- Niko Njotorahardjo *(Indonesia)*
- Opoku Onyinah *(Ghana)*
- Michel Ouedraogo *(Burkina Faso)*
- Nick Park *(Ireland)*
- Oreste Pesare *(ICCRS)*
- Phil Pringle *(C3)*
- Mike Rakes *(USA)*
- Gordon Robertson *(CBN)*
- Samuel Rodriguez *(NHCLC)*

- Edson Rebustini *(Brazil)*
- Goodwill Shana *(Zimbabwe)*
- Ed Stetzer *(USA)*
- Steve Strang *(Charisma)*
- Greg Surratt *(USA)*
- Vinson Synan *(ORU)*
- Matthew Thomas *(India)*
- Jean-Luc Trachsel *(Switzerland)*
- Kenneth Ulmer *(USA)*
- Gilberto Velez *(NHCLC)*
- Todd White *(Lifestyle Christianity)*
- Stovall Weems *(USA)*
- David Wells *(Canada)*
- David Zongo *(Switzerland)*
- Caleb Wehrli *(USA)*
- Billy Wilson *(ORU)*
- George Wood *(World AOG)*

For more information, visit: **JERUSALEM2020.COM**

 SPONSORS:

TABLE OF CONTENTS

Three Essential Spiritual Relationships | Kenneth Ulmer 9
Sent to Win the Nations | César Castellanos 17
The Year of the Voice | Cindy Jacobs 25
Working Together for the Harvest | Heidi Baker 33
Called to be Harvesters | Jean-Luc Trachsel 41
The Third Pentecost | Niko Njotorahardjo 45
Innovation and Disruption | Rob Hoskins 51
Breaking the Sound Barrier | Russell Evans 61
Be Holy, Be One, Be Light | Samuel Rodriguez 69
A Holistic Revival | Stovall Weems 73
The World Through Four Lenses | Todd Johnson 79
How to Fail (Or Succeed) | George Wood 87
The Everyday Believer | Andy Byrd 97
A Paradigm Shift | Billy Wilson 107
Praying for a Double Portion | Paul Dhinakaran 117
A Friend of Israel | Jentezen Franklin 123
The Key to Successful Evangelism | Michael Koulianos 131
Men Like Trees Walking | Nathan Morris 137
What Do I See in 2020? | Goodwill Shana 147
A Commission for Everyone | Chadwick Mohan 149
Every Tongue, Tribe, and Nation | Ed Stetzer 155
Jerusalem2020 Speakers 163

THREE ESSENTIAL SPIRITUAL RELATIONSHIPS

Kenneth Ulmer

A great prophet asked the question, "Can two walk—journey, do life together—unless they be agreed?" This prophet lifts up the essential issue of the value of true, committed relationships. In the next few pages, I want to explore with you at least three relationships you must always have in your life. Number one is you must always have a father. Number two is you must always have a son or a daughter. Number three is you're going to need a friend. A father, a son or daughter, and a friend.

I was blessed to have two spiritual fathers. I am from the spiritual loins of Dr. Melvin Wade, from Mount Moriah Baptist Church, as well as a great giant, Bishop Benjamin Reid, who is now with the Lord. Bishop Reid handled me, looked at me, regarded me, and loved me as a father.

Paul poses an interesting statement in 1 Corinthians 4:15. He says, "For though you have countless guides in Christ, you do not have many fathers. For I became your father in Christ Jesus through the gospel." Who fathers you? Who parents you in the ministry? Who is your overseer? Who do you allow into your life closely enough that they see and relate to you as a son or as a daughter? Who are your fathers?

I hope you literally pray for a father. I hope you put that on your prayer list. Pray, "Lord, send me a father. Send me a mother. Send me a parent. Send me a spiritually mature man or woman of God to cover me."

When Bishop Reid went to be with the Lord, it was an extremely painful time for me. Other sons of Bishop Reid's came from all over the country. I'll never forget the great celebration of the life of this great man. I had preached at his retirement, before he died—a message about Elijah and Elisha, and their relationship of mentor and mentee—father and son—and multi-generational ministry. And at the end of that message, I'll never forget what I did. I got down on my knees and I asked Bishop Reid, in front of thousands of people, to give me a double anointing of the call of God on his life.

Oh, I know we can't duplicate. We can't become cookie cutters. However, this gesture was an expression of how close I felt to this man. There, in front of that great audience, Bishop Reid laid his hands on me and he prayed for me. Most importantly of all, he did this as a father.

A few weeks later, I saw a friend of mine who was also one of his sons. We were talking about how hard it had been to lose the Bishop, and how we were coping since pop had left. This friend said, "Man, how are you doing?"

I replied, "I'm having a hard time."

He said, "Come on. How are you doing?"

I explained it this way—maybe you'll gain a new understanding of the value of fatherhood when I tell you this. I said, "Man, I feel like I'm walking in the rain without an umbrella.

I feel uncovered. I feel unprotected. I feel like I'm out here all by myself."

I've got friends. I've got colleagues. I've got people whom I stand before every Sunday—hundreds, maybe thousands of people. But there was this void when my spiritual father went to be with the Lord. I felt like I was walking in the rain without an umbrella. We have many, many teachers, but not many fathers.

Another example of a spiritual father is seen in the relationship between Paul and Timothy. Paul writes two letters to his son, Timothy. In each of these letters, he validates, emphasizes, and clarifies that he's writing to Timothy as a son: "Timothy, my beloved son." Paul talks about Timothy's spiritual journey, and the impact of his mother and grandmother. In the second letter, Paul coaches him, if you will. He guides him in how to be a young pastor at the church at Ephesus. Still, he calls Timothy, "My beloved son."

You need a father after whom to pattern your life. Paul literally poured his life into Timothy. And many believe that, historically, Paul wrote to Timothy from a jail cell, while chained to a Roman soldier. Still, he wrote to encourage his son. Timothy was a priority, even despite the challenges in his own life.

Paul always had a relational, multi-generational perspective on what it meant to be in ministry. He said to Timothy, "I've taught you and poured into you—now take those lessons and share, pour into others, and teach other faithful men, so that they can share it, too." Spiritual fathers are in multi-generational relationships. Paul is looking down the road towards his spiritual grandsons. He's looking at what the dynamics of ministry are really all about.

ABLAZE—A PROPHETIC CALL TO IGNITE THE CHURCH

We get the impression that his letter to Timothy was, perhaps, a response—similar to the letter to the Corinthians. With the latter, Paul corrected and answered questions to deal with disturbances in the church. Paul writes as a soon-to-retire general to this young neophyte, this lieutenant. He tells him about his journeys in the leadership of the kingdom of God. He keeps coming back to that idea of Timothy being a son. He says, "Son, some of them will not hear you. Some of them will reject you. Though, don't let them despise your youth. Walk with integrity. Stick with the words. Stick with the word." You know that famous passage, preach the word in season and out season? This is Paul's exhortation to his spiritual son.

It's a father who can tell you that, when you get in trouble, you'd better preach that word. The reality is that preaching that word will, at times, get you in trouble. On the flip side, the same preaching that gets you in trouble at times will also get you out of trouble at other times. So Paul says to this son, "Son, stay with the Word. Be a good soldier." He encourages Timothy in the relationship between himself and his God, but also in the relationship between Timothy and Paul as father and son.

WHO IS YOUR SPIRITUAL FATHER?

Better yet, who's your son? Who's your daughter? Into whom are you pouring your life? What will the next generation receive from you? What's coming down from generation to generation, from father to son? Look back over your shoulder, to your father who has poured into you. Again, ministry has a multidimensional nature.

Who is your son, whom you can confront and love? Who is your son, to whom you can speak the truth in love? Who is your son, who, when you see him going off the trail, allows you to have a relationship in which you talk to him about it? Who trusts you enough to allow you to be their father?

Paul called Timothy his beloved son. You can almost feel the bond between this man and this young pastor. Paul pours out his heart, and Timothy loves him enough to receive his counsel.

Some of your sons won't receive your counsel. Some of your daughters won't hear you. Isn't it interesting that, when the prodigal son came to his father and said, "Give me my stuff. I'm out of here," the father never tried to talk him out of it? Instead, he gave him what he wanted and allowed him to go off on his own.

Sometimes your sons and daughters will not hear you. Sometimes the people into whom you've poured your life will not respond, will not love you enough to trust you. It's a reality. It's a dilemma that you will face as a father to a son. It's a challenge that you will face as a son to a father.

Paul loved Timothy. Timothy loved Paul. You cannot choose your blood sons, your blood daughters. They're your children. But God gifts spiritual fathers to sons and spiritual sons to fathers, and they must be mutually received. And so, as you read this letter, you can almost see Timothy reading Paul's writing. You can almost hear Timothy saying, "Yes dad. Yes dad. Yes, yes, yes, yes. And what about this dad? What about that dad?" You always need a father after whom to pattern your life. You always need a son or a daughter into whom to pour your life. The next generation is looking to you.

Thirdly, you need a friend to pray for. You need a friend to pray for you. John wrote the books of John, 1 John,

ABLAZE—A PROPHETIC CALL TO IGNITE THE CHURCH

2 John, 3 John, and Revelation. In one of his shortest letters—the Johns—he writes to his friend Gaius, and says, "My beloved friend. My beloved friend." This is not a son. This is not a father. He identifies him, over and over, as a beloved friend.

Ask yourself this question: If you have just received a blessing—some good news, something amazing that's happened to you—and you've seen the hand of God do it. . .who would be the first person you call? Put a pin in that.

Phase 2: You fall. You sin. You yield to the attack of the enemy. It's greatest fall of your life. The worst choice you've ever made. The worst thing that's ever happened to you. Now who do you call? Truly think about that for a minute. So here are the two questions: You get the best news—who would you call? Other side: You get the worst news—who do you call? Ideally, it's the same person. Ideally, there's someone in your life who walks so close to you that you fully trust them, even if they're not a blood relative or someone who's been with you all your life. This person, this friend, is a gift from God into your life. This is why Paul calls Gaius his beloved friend.

You don't really need a friend when you're up. You can make it when you're right. I don't need anybody with me when I'm right. I need somebody with me when I'm in the wrong—when I don't know what's right. That's a real friend. A real friend looks not for perfection but for commitment. You need a friend to pray for, and who will pray for you. Who's on your prayer list? Who do you call? Who have you allowed into your life enough to pray for you?

One of the buzzwords now is "accountability partner." I've discovered that most "accountability partners" are just associates. There's very little accountability in what most people call accountability, because you let a real accountable friend into your personal business. Who can ask you about how you spend your money? Who's close enough to you to ask you about how you're treating your wife? Who can confront you about the girl that you flirted with? Who can confront you about the eyes and the looks that you give someone else? That's a real friend.

You need a friend to pray for you. You need a friend to pray for. You need a son to pour your life into. You need a daughter to share your life with. And you need a father to pattern your life after.

Timothy wanted to be like Paul. Who are you patterning your life after? Who has God sent you? Who has God given into your life as a father? Who has God given into your life as a son or a daughter? Who has God given into your life as a friend? I pray that you would have one of each.

SENT TO WIN THE NATIONS

César Castellanos

In Genesis 12:2, the Lord said to Abraham, "I will make you a great nation. I will bless you and make your name great and you shall be a blessing." When we come to know Jesus as our Lord, not only do we receive his calling, but he also gives us the purpose for which we are in this world.

God revealed himself to Abraham when Abraham was 75 years old. From that point onward, Abraham understood the purpose for which the Lord had called him. Now, every single one of us can experience this same thing when we have a true personal encounter with Jesus. I came to know Jesus when I was 18 years old, because of a philosophy professor I had in school. During every single one of his classes, he would always speak with a Bible in his hand. He attacked everything sacred about the Bible—the deity of Jesus, the mystery of Trinity, and the veracity of the text.

Now, I knew that he was wrong, but I had no way of proving it. One day, he was pointing at the Bible, and he said, "Not only have I read this book, but I have studied it." In my heart, there was a challenge. I said to myself, "If that atheist has read the Bible and studied it, why can't I? I'm going to study it. I'll read it and prove to him that he's wrong." That same day, I went back home and I looked for a Bible, and I began to read it. I thought to myself, "A book. Well, you have to read it from the start." I began from the book of Genesis, and every single day, I was reading several chapters of the Bible. I did this for nine months.

I'd read the entire Old Testament and the four gospels, but yet I did not know Jesus. One day, I had a thought: I'd like to have an appointment with God; so I prayed a prayer. I said, "Lord, I'd like to have an appointment with you. I'll see you tomorrow. I'll be waiting for you at 10:30 PM in the living room." I chose 10:30 PM because I knew my family would be asleep. The next day, at 10:30 PM sharp, I was in my living room. I sat there waiting on the Lord. I kept the lights off. I kept the sound off. I prayed a short little prayer and said to him, "Lord Jesus, I don't know you. I don't know who you are, but if you are truly the God of the Bible, the God Almighty that I've been reading about, I want you to do something in me. Change me, and change me now."

I kept silent. I didn't know much about prayer; but I realized that if I asked for something, I should wait for an answer. In the spiritual world, it felt like there was a lot of pressure. There were many thoughts coming and going in my mind. Later, I understood that they were thoughts of the enemy. For instance, I'd heard a voice saying to me, "Who do you think you are, that you would speak to God that way? God is not interested in you. You are nothing." I thought in response, "Well, I don't care. If he is God, he will answer." Fifteen minutes passed, and something amazing happened. I was staring at the front door of my house, which was made of stained glass, and I saw a very bright light passing in front of my door. It came all the way to where I was, and I knew that in that light was Jesus.

The size of that light was like the size of a person. It came and it stopped right next to me. As soon as I felt the presence of God beside me, everything within me began to burn. I felt a heat. I could feel a fire burning on the inside, and all of a sudden, I felt that I was suspended between heaven and earth and I was able to see the glory of God. I saw Him. He was so high—higher than the heavens; so deep—deeper than the oceans; and so wide—wider than the seven seas. I felt like a little insect, and I felt convicted of my sin. In that moment, everything concealed in me began to surface. I said, "Lord, get away from me. I am not worthy of you. I am a sinner, and I repent Lord. I have done this and this and that." I confessed every one of my sins.

When I finished, I saw a hand penetrating my head. It descended down to the soles of my feet. It felt like a caress. It was the most beautiful feeling I have ever felt in my life. God was caressing me, and He cleansed me from all my sins—from all evil in me. He filled me with a joy—a supernatural joy. I could not bear to keep sitting. I fell onto my knees, and lifted my hands to heaven. I began to worship Him with all the strength of my soul. When I got up from my knees, I said to the Lord, "Lord, if this is what you give, you will find me here every day. I will seek you." Since that moment, I have understood that something happened in my life. I was born again, and I left all the vices in my life.

I left all my friends. Everything within me was changed. I didn't realize why until later, when I understood that Jesus was now living in my heart. Because I had never been to a Christian church, I would take two-hour walks and talk to Jesus. I did this for a while, and became strong in my spirit. One day, the Lord led me to a small church, where I heard they were worshiping God. When I looked inside, it seemed so ridiculous to me that I thought, "This is not for me." I was going to walk away, but I felt something that stopped me. I heard a voice saying, "You're not going anywhere. You're going in there."

I walked in. Yes, it was a Christian group, and I heard the preaching of the Word of God, which I enjoyed. I decided to keep on coming back. Shortly thereafter, I had an experience with the Holy Spirit and I kept on growing in my faith. The Lord began to guide me, step by step, in everything I needed to do. I got involved in a Christian church that was well-established and then I became the president of the youth group.

Shortly after that, the Lord led me to pastor a church. I pastored churches for nine years—small churches of maybe up to 120 members. The last church that I pastored before I began Mission Charismatic International was a church in which there were approximately 30 people. After one year, we were able to grow to 120. However, it was as if there were a back door in the church through which people were leaving. I felt a little bit frustrated at this. I said to the Lord, "If this is what it is to pastor—to win people and lose them—I don't like this. I'm going to resign being the pastor, and I'm not going to commit to do anything unless you speak to me."

Four months later, I was on holidays with my family, visiting the coast of Columbia. One afternoon, I went to the beach to talk to God. I sat down in a little rocking chair, and began to pray. In that moment, the presence of God came in such a supernatural way that the Lord began to speak to me. He gave me a dream of a very large church, because dreams are the language of my spirit. He said, "The church you will pastor will be so numerous, it will be like the stars in the heavens, like the sand in the sea. It will be a countless multitude." Then, the Lord asked me what kind of church I would like to pastor. I stared at the ground, wondering why God had mentioned sand. I asked, "What is it about sand? I can't see anything special about sand."

All of a sudden, I had a vision in which I saw every grain of sand transformed into a person. I began to visualize hundreds of thousands of people. The Lord asked me, "What are you looking at?" I said, "Lord, I see hundreds of thousands of people." The Lord said to me, "Well, that and much more I will give to you if you walk in my perfect will." The Lord said, "Look, you need to have your priorities in order. Number one is God. Many people believe in Me, but very few live their lives in love with Me." He continued, "The number two priority is you, because you are a channel through which My Spirit flows." I understood that I needed to take care of my mind, my emotions, and my will. Thirdly, God said, "'Your family is your third priority. It needs to be an example, a model. The fourth priority is the ministry, and the fifth priority is your secular job."

A month after God gave that word to me, we gave birth to a church called Mission Charismatic International. It started with eight people in the living room of our home. Though I had a great vision in my heart, I did not know how to do the work. When we came to have 20 or 25 people in our service, I said, "Lord, I need you to give me a goal. I have a great big goal, but I need a short-term goal." In a vision, I saw the number 200. I said, "Wow, that's a great goal!" 200 people. I wrote that number down in different places so I could see it.

I wrote a deadline: the 19th of September, 1983. It was a six-month goal; three months later, I started to see that the Lord was really answering my prayer. So many people started coming. So many people visited that many could not come in. They had to wait outside in line. Six months later, we had achieved our goal—the vision that God had given me. I started setting other goals, and it continued in the same way. We did this until we came to the point of having to move to bigger venues. Eventually, we ended up renting a coliseum every weekend for the multitudes. We came to the point of having seven services in the weekends in that coliseum, and then we bought a building of our own, which has capacity for 11,000 people. Today, we have seven services there every single weekend.

We've also opened many different branches in other cities in our nation. It all began with having a vision. We started receiving visits from many different people from around the world—people who wanted to learn the principles God had given us. We taught them how to work in people's houses, and reproduce through cell groups that empowered people for leadership. God allowed me to start teaching in so many different nations. We have seen that people embrace the principles, and are producing such abundant fruit. God does this not because he has preferences for a particular person or people; He wants to use anyone who is willing to be used by Him in a supernatural way.

The Lord said to His apostles, "Go therefore all over the world and make disciples of all nations." The Lord sent his servants, his disciples, not to win people in nations, but to win nations. That is exactly what we're seeing today. We are seeing nations turning back to the Lord, with hearts fully opened and committed to Him. I know that God makes no exceptions. He is looking for men and women who will hear His voice—people who are willing to obey Him so that He can use them. I'm so grateful to God for the opportunity of sharing with each and every one of you.

I want to tell you that you are not going to be the exception. God wants to use you in such a supernatural way. There's no time to waste. We need to take advantage of every moment to influence people's lives. Every single one of us must say to Him, "Lord, here am I, send me."

Father, I'm so grateful for every person that's reading this message. I pray that your hand be upon them, that you bless them in a supernatural way. Lord, I pray that you open the floodgates of heaven and fill them with your power and authority so that they open their mouths to proclaim your truth. May your grace, glory, and power flow through them. Lord, I pray that you do this. Amen.

THE YEAR OF THE VOICE

Cindy Jacobs

I'm really excited to bring you the word of the Lord. We just finished a meeting for 2020 with a group from the Global Prophetic Movement—people from 42 nations. We gleaned so many things from this meeting—much more than I'm going to be able to give in this short time with you. I'm going to share some life-changing things to help you as you transition from 2019 to 2020.

2019 was the year we set for joyful increase. Many people have told me they believe that, and that they did see an increase—financially, career-wise, or in a new house. Perhaps it wasn't that way for everyone; but I would say, in general, that we are still in that season of increase.

2020 is significant, in that it is literally a new era. Some of the words God has given me—not personally, but also for others—include that we're going to grow into our own skin. What do I mean by that? We're going to grow into the purposes that God has for us. It's time to intentionally say, "What is my purpose? Where am I going in life, and how do I achieve that? How do I come into a convergence, where my full gifts, my full abilities, are used?" It's a very exciting season.

Of course it will be a challenging season as well. Any time you're going to go a new level, you'll encounter new devils. There will be some resistance. Think about when the Israelites went into the Promised Land: there was resistance—giants who met them. If you're going into your Promised Land—your purpose, your destiny, that which you're supposed to do in life, that God has for you—and you're not having any pushback, then you're not going the right direction. There will be Jerichos to take. There will be battles, but it's going to be exciting when you're going the way the Lord has for you. There is that surety inside of you—a sense that this is what you were made for. You've been created to do this.

I want to give you hope for your future. Maybe you've gone through terrible times of loss, or times in which you had setbacks. But I want to say to you, believe God. Believe God that He does have something wonderful for you. No matter how many things have happened to you, how much loss, this is a year where we are literally starting not only a new decade, but a new era.

It is a year of the voice. Now, why do I say that? 2 Chronicles 20:20 says, this says, "So they rose early in the morning when in the wilderness to Cohen and they went out. Jehoshaphat stood and said, 'Hear me, O Judah, and you inhabitants of Jerusalem; believe in the Lord and you will be established; believe his prophets and you shall prosper.'" Then, it goes on to talk about something very critical for this season: "And when he had consulted with the people, he appointed those who should sing to the Lord, who should praise the beauty of holiness. And they went out before the army and were saying, 'Praise the Lord, for his mercy endures forever.'" So we say that this is a season in which we're going to have to go to war.

If we could look at the biblical symbolism of taking your Promised Land, we see that, when the children of Israel crossed over the Jordan River, there were all kinds of tests they had to go through. They didn't just stand on the Promised Land soil and say, "Here I am." All the giants didn't immediately run away; all the problems didn't magically disappear. No, they had to fight for it. This is a season in which we're going to have to go to war in order to come into our reset and our blessings and our purpose. Don't let that make you afraid. Simply learn how to go to war. This is extremely important. At Generals International, we teach on spiritual warfare, and we tell people how to navigate, in prayer, the powers of darkness coming against them.

We need to go back and reteach those things that we taught many years ago. One of the things my generation should do is teach the next generation what we know. For instance, my generation knew how to go to war. We haven't had physical wars as much in the last few years. We've had terrorist attacks, and we've certainly had people deployed; but it's not a world war, or a full-scale war.

We need to understand that there are nations that need Jesus Christ—there's going to be a battle over that. There are people who need to be saved—there's going to be a battle for the souls of those people. So it's time to establish war rooms once again; it's time to learn how to go to war. In 2 Chronicles, we see that one of the principles of warfare was worship.

We know, in this 2020 season, that there will be a blessing connected to our intense worship of the Lord. This is the 20th year of the Episodic Council of prophetic elders. We first began to have meetings in 1999, and we're seeing that the prophetic movement in 2020 is coming into a fullness. Many are learning to prophesy around the world, learning about cooperating with the Holy Spirit, and learning how to hear the voice of God. We especially see this in the growth of evangelism. It's so exciting!

There are many other groups of prophets, of course. However, our particular group felt that we should give a cautionary word—that we needed to once again issue some guidelines on prophecy. For instance, discouraging people from telling others who to marry, when to make a move, and things like that. My book, *The Voice of God*, is a good place to begin if you're just learning about prophecy. Many other leaders, such as Bishop Bill Hammond, have written books on the prophetic, as well. And so we see this fullness coming, and we see that the prophetic is going to rise up in many spheres of authority. That's important to know as well—there's going to be marketplace prophets.

We were just talking to one the other day, who was telling us how, when he's with a group of business people, he gets very detailed words. There are others as well, who are this kind of prophet. We know there are some of us who will sing the word of the Lord. In this case, it would be exactly what needs to be heard. Another thing that we heard, in this year of the voice, is that, in this new era, we need to let our voices be heard and established around the world. Here are some ways we can do just that.

1. A Voice of Warning

This is similar to a watchman sounding the alarm. If you are feeling something coming that is dangerous to your nation or another—let's say you had a dream—many times, that's God telling you that you need to pray about that thing.

2. A Voice of Righteousness

3. Increase guidance given through the prophets to leaders.

There are governmental prophets rising up, and it's very exciting. In fact, it's a common occurrence for me to speak to world leaders and to give them prophetic counsel.

4. A Decrease in Proclamation

5. Wise Choices in What We Preach

I saw a vision of the word "Watch." The Lord told me that He was going to confirm that we were going to have more intercessors—more rooms—and that we'll be able to watch and be Watchmen.

At our global prophetic summit, the Lord actually gave us a sign of this during the first night. A woman who was legally blind was completely healed, and she was able to see. She stood about ten feet away, and I held up fingers. I moved further and further back, and she could still see. I was holding up two fingers, then five fingers. I really felt that this was a confirmation of what God is going to do. This year, we're seeing miracles as we watch over the nations. This is a time of very strong violence in the heavens. As we look at nations, we see that there's violence on and in the earth, as well.

I see, in the U.S. and other countries, that there will be more and more clashes that rise up. We need to pray about this. In fact, if we pray about them, we can quell them, and they don't necessarily have to happen. I see people becoming very heated with one another. Regardless of how you feel politically, there needs to be civility; the Holy Spirit can help us discuss the issues with respect for one another—even disagree without getting angry or using derogatory speech. I think that we can be Christlike in how we're sharing. We are in a Jesus movement, and the love of the lost is breaking out.

It's very interesting, as we look around the world, how many nations are having godly government rise up in connection with Israel. Prophetically, God is giving more and more of His people a love for the middle East and the middle Eastern people—those in the Muslim world, both Arabic and non-Arabic-speaking peoples.

God is going to move and we're going to see many people come to the Lord—millions! There's going to be an increase of evangelism in a great way—greater than we can imagine or dream. Another thing the Lord showed us is that chorus miracles are going to keep playing a greater part, even like we saw the legally blind lady healed at the global prophetic summit. There were other miracles that happened there as well.

As we were praying at the GPC consultation with 42 nations, we felt like there was almost a roar that we heard—the sound of many waters coming together. We were going hear this roar in worship. We were going to hear it. There will be more and more agreement, as many prophetic streams come together, as well as great authority to make decrees that will change governments.

This is an expectation the Lord has strongly given me: God doesn't simply want us prophesy the problems from the earth; but He gives us the ability to see heavenly solutions from His perspective. This is a year, a season, of reset. This is the day we will be anointed for reset. This reset will bring a breakthrough for relations for families, for the nation. God is going to turn impossible situations around. That's an exciting word for 2020, isn't it?

WORKING TOGETHER FOR THE HARVEST

Heidi Baker

What do you think God is doing in 2020 with the church?

I believe that this year, in the body of Christ, there's been a lot of shaking and preparation. There's a movement of God that is breathing on the earth; He is raising people up to stand and to go for it in the kingdom of God. I really believe that this is people being released, and we are going to see a harvest of God. It's not going to be easy; but I really believe that God has been preparing and breathing on what he wants to do on the nations.

So I believe 2020 is the year of harvest—the greatest harvest we've ever seen. I believe God is uniting churches and church leaders to support one another. I believe that churches are going to hold up the net together for the fishes coming in. So as the church is going out, and people are coming in, churches are going to start supporting each other and being united—the leadership for the people.

God is going to use his people. God is going to use these Harvesters, all over the world, to bring in this great harvest. It's not just one nation that He's touching—it's the nations of the planet.

ABLAZE—A PROPHETIC CALL TO IGNITE THE CHURCH

The Lord's after His bride. 2020's going to be the best year we've ever seen. There's going to be supernatural vision: many things that have been held back are going to be released in 2020. I believe that it's the year God's going to do something major with evangelism, something major with His heart to reach the nations. What does this look like? As the body of Christ, we are meant to work together. Sometimes, we think we've got the solution, right? However, if we think we're doing it on our own, that's misguided. If we think that we are the end-all-be-all—that we've got it all together, we're mistaken. We cannot do this on our own.

As the Lord is calling us to go reach the planet, to reach every single man, woman, and child on this planet, what needs to happen? Power, love, gifting and character. Sometimes, we see power without character. We see love without power. Love without power is wimpy. We don't want that kind of love—that's like being toothless. We want love and power to come together with character. It looks like us learning how to work together with the body of Christ. We can't do it without Singapore. We can't do it without China. We can't do it without all of the body in Asia coming together with us. We can't do it without the Western bride. We can't do it without the Middle Eastern Bride. We can't do it without the Arab bride, and the Israeli bride. We need each other to carry this gospel. We need each other.

Here is the vision I received as we were praying with our movement, our leaders. We were praying for the power of God to fall, and for God to speak to us. What do you think happened? God crashed this meeting—we were under the table, the whole bunch of the leaders, crying, wrecked, undone. And I saw a powerful vision of a net coming down. I thought, "Yes, Lord. This is strategy for our movement. I'm so excited.

Yes Lord, you're going to download it to me." And the Lord laughed. He said, "Sweetheart, that's your movement." And he showed me this little piece of the net. It was a massive net I saw coming down from heaven. He said, "That's your movement there." I said, "What?" He said, "That's your movement."

Then I had an impression of angels weaving together the body of Yeshua. He showed me these angels weaving together with silver and golden cords. And He said, "That's the assemblies of God. That's the Catholics." I said, "What?" He said, "That's the Catholics, that's the Baptists, that's the Campus Crusade." I mean, He went through lists. "That's YWAM. Oh, there, that's Bethel. Oh, that's Catch the Fire. That's…" On and on He went, showing me all these movements. He said, "Unless the body of Christ works together, then we will lose the harvest."

That's what I feel about 2020. We need to work together—all of us—to bring in the harvest of God.

What happened to me when I fell in love with the body of Christ? The body of Christ started inviting me to come and speak. The twenty years before this, I'd had no invitations except from Fairbanks, Alaska, in the winter, and one tiny church in Mexico. Why the lack of invitations? Because I'd had this edge. I didn't like the church body. I thought they didn't care about the poor, the dying, the sick, the broke, the slaves. God told me, "I'm calling you to love the church. I'm calling you to love the people I want you to love. Because I love My church. I love My bride. I love My people. And unless you love them, you have no authority."

That's an important point. You have no authority where you have no love. And where you have love, you have authority. There are real divisions in churches over politics. How is that possible? Are we a political movement, or are we the body of Christ? If somebody thinks differently than you do politically, can you somehow push them away like they're not part of the body? If they're lovers of Yeshua, then they are your brother or your sister. It doesn't matter what party people belong to; what matters is that they are lovers of Jesus. And if you love them, you have authority. Without love, you have no authority.

God is calling the body of Yeshua to come together with great, incredible love, and to use that net—which is every single movement on the planet—to gather the harvest. We want you to be a people filled up with the Lamb's love, filled up with the presence of God, and burning brightly, forever and ever and ever.

The Lord showed me that it matters how you look at things. God wants to open our eyes in regards to His people. God loves Israel. He loves everyone; and He wants us to share that heart.

When I was in my home in Mozambique, I could literally walk across my yard and go into the ocean. One day, I walked out, and the Lord said to me, "I want you to go face down." So there I am, with my mask and snorkel, ready to go seek the Lord. He said, "It's as easy to step into the kingdom as it is for you to go face down into the water. It's as easy for you to see kingdom reality as it is for you to go face down into the water. But you have to lose control. You have to believe that I can show you another reality."

As I went face down, I saw the coral, the fish—an entirely different world under that water. Now, everybody walking on the land can see the ocean; but unless you go face down into it, you can't see what's underneath the surface. The Lord said to me, "I want to take you into a kingdom reality. I want to take you into a holy harvest place; but you're going to have to go face down. You're going to have to step into another reality, release control, and be in My glory."

I was in this place, just floating, and I started to cry. My mask was fogged with my tears. I was undone by the presence of God, looking into the water into a different reality. This matters for you, too. In order to fulfill God's call on your life, you'll need this tenacity. You'll need patience and endurance, but these come from being in a face down posture. They come from laying your life down every day, and giving it all, and saying, "God, I want to see what You see, do what You do, go where You go." So as I am pondering all of this, I'm still face down in the water. The Lord speaks to me as clearly as anything: "Heidi, build a university."

Can you imagine? I'd had years of being mocked in school environments. In university, when I would try to spell, the teachers would wonder, "How did you get in here? You can't spell." They couldn't understand my challenges. And so when He told me to do that, it totally, completely shocked me. I sucked water into my snorkel; I started choking. And I knew that I knew that I knew that I had to do something in that moment.

This is where I want you to be right now. Wake up! This is the challenge. This is what I want to call you to right here, right now. What happened when the Lord spoke to me was that I had to get out of the water and do something. Right now, what are you going to do next? You can't just receive what God has given you to do and say to yourself, "It doesn't matter. Just let it die. I'm going to forget that in three months." Step out of the water. Step out of the water, and do what God's called you to do. Go back in everyday, into the secret place. He's going to put things on your heart. What do you do when God gives you a calling?

Obey.

Step out.

Trust.

Prepare.

See, when I did my PhD, I didn't understand why. God had called me to the poor. I'd been working with the poor all my Christian life. Why on earth would God ask me to go do a PhD—ten years of education? Because He knew that day I'd be in the water, and He'd tell me to go and build a university; and you need a PhD to do that. Some of the things God will tell you to do, you won't immediately understand. Why does the Lord want you to become an engineer? Why does the Lord want you to learn a certain language? Why has God called you to the family that you're in right now?

God knows everything. He knows exactly how you were raised, and where He put you. He is not disabling you; He is using you for His glory. I stepped out of that water, and you know what the Lord said? "Go and build first grade." I stepped out of the water, I put on clothes, I went to the base. I literally just dried myself out and went to the base. And I went to a tree, a big old tree, an Imbondeiro tree. I took a stick. I got some of my friends around—we didn't have any money. We had no teachers. I said, "This is a first grade class. Does anyone know how to read?" I found someone who knew. I said, "Do any children want to study?" Lots of kids wanted to study.

I had them teach something that day. And I said, "Tomorrow, officially, first grade class starts."

For however long it took, we had first grade class under that tree. As soon as the Lord provided money for bamboo sticks, we bought bamboo sticks. And as soon as the Lord provided money for rocks, we got rocks. As soon as the Lord provided money for a sack of cement, we stuck cement over the sticks and the rocks. And that's what we did, and we kept doing that and doing that, and doing that until we started building with blocks. And then we started building with pillars. And we just kept going until what started under a little tree became 3500 students, the best school by far, in the nation of Mozambique.

That's what happened. Glory to God. The vision is not made in a day. It took twelve years to build all the way to 12th grade. God is asking you, like in Habakkuk 2, to write some things down—to make it plain. What is the Lord calling you to do? Go for it.

CALLED TO BE HARVESTERS

Jean-Luc Trachsel

Hello my friend, I'm Jean-Luc Trachsel from Switzerland. I'm the president of The International Association of Healing Ministries, which works around the globe. I have the privilege of seeing how God is moving in a powerful way today. I also have the great joy and privilege of co-leading the Global Evangelist Alliance with Daniel Kolenda and that's connected and partnered fully with Empowered21.

I believe in this vision and mission: that before 2033, the Holy Spirit will come in demonstration and power, and will touch every human being on this planet, that everyone may have an encounter with Jesus through the Spirit. This is exactly what Joel prophesied years ago: that in the last days, there will be an outpouring of the Holy Spirit. My friends, I really believe we are in the last days. I believe, as we are seeing around the globe, there is turmoil, earthquake, wars, and many bad things.

But the other way we can see it—and I'm seeing this perspective as I'm traveling worldwide—is that God is in control, and He is moving like never before. He is pouring out his Spirit upon all flesh, because the Holy Spirit is not just for a certain group of people. The Holy Spirit is for everyone, because the work of the Holy Spirit is to reveal Jesus. I believe there is a

Jesus movement arising, where people around the world are hungry and thirsty—not just for religion or denomination—but for God! The Holy Spirit is revealing to this generation Jesus, the only Savior, the only Law—the Healer and Deliverer.

I'm so excited to be part of Empowered21, and to be part of this historic gathering in Jerusalem from May 31 to June 3, 2020. I encourage you to be part of that—it's going to be historic, as people from different denominations and nations go to Jerusalem to fulfill the prophecy. God will visit us. Israel is connected directly to the plan of God for these last days. Be part of that! Open yourself up. I want to encourage all of us to quit the old-fashioned way of defending our flags and denominations—of thinking in the box. Today, I believe the Lord is challenging us to come out of the box—to preach the ABC's of the gospel, to gather not just to fill up our own churches, but to bring the kingdom of heaven to this generation with a demonstration of power. And this demonstration of power can happen only through the Holy Spirit. That is the reason the Holy Spirit is my best, best friend. I encourage you to welcome Him into your life as your best friend. He's going to teach you, help you, strengthen you, and empower you to fulfill your mission.

It's not about stars. It's not about one preacher traveling around the world. It's about a movement of disciples who love Jesus, who are serving Jesus, and who are offering God's Word to the mission fields of today. I want to encourage you to open your eyes and see the harvest. It is ready, everywhere. As I'm traveling, I can see it in America; in Europe especially, because I'm working here; but also in Asia, Africa, and Australia. The harvest is white, but the Lord needs harvesters; and that's the reason he's calling you by name. He has chosen you and wants to establish you, that you may go to preach the gospel. Where is your mission field?

A new mission field today is the marketplace. What a wonderful privilege you have, if it's your call to bring the gospel with a demonstration of power to the bank, to the marketplace, to the business field. That's fantastic. Maybe you are called to be a medical doctor or nurse. That's fantastic, because God is looking for harvesters to go into the medical field, and He wants to equip you to reach the unreached. You can manifest the kingdom of heaven with a true demonstration of power. Maybe you are called to the sports field; to become a secretary or a teacher; to be a social worker—or whatever the Lord is calling you to. Maybe it's a place He's calling you to: a country or a city; but one sure thing is that the Lord has chosen you. You can bring the gospel with a true demonstration of power to the place where you are, to touch your family, your friends, and your neighbors.

This is the harvest time. This is where God is going to reveal Himself to this generation. May the Lord bless you abundantly and more than ever. If you're Mennonite, a Baptist, a Catholic, Orthodox—whatever your denomination may be—the most important thing for all of us is to put our faith and trust in Jesus, and ask Him to baptize us with His flame of fire—with His Holy Spirit. May the Lord bless you abundantly. I would love to pray for you, that the Holy Spirit may visit you today.

Lord God, thanks so much that, at the age of five, I gave my life to you. At the age of six, in a simple way, when I was in my pajamas in my living room, you came upon me with this flame of fire and you baptized me with the strong power of the Holy Spirit.

ABLAZE—A PROPHETIC CALL TO IGNITE THE CHURCH

I pray for the viewers today, that you can visit them in the name of Jesus. Father, you said that if we ask you anything, you will give it to us. I ask you to give the Holy Spirit—to pour out Your Spirit upon all those reading this today. Holy Spirit, come upon them with a flame of fire, so that they can bring the gospel with energy—with a fire in which people can see Jesus, alive. I pray that you live inside of them to bring about the fruits that you carry, so that we can be equipped to go to the harvest fields with the gifts of prophecy, wisdom, intelligence, healings, miracles, faith, and praying in tongues.

I pray that those who have never been baptized in the Holy Spirit would be baptized right now; for those who have, I pray a fresh anointing—that they would start speaking in tongues because, as my dear friend has told me many times, speaking in tongues is the highway to touch the atmosphere of heaven—the kingdom of heaven. So just pray in tongues where you are, and as you pray in tongues, the Holy Spirit is coming with you, with a fresh anointing, in Jesus's name. May the Lord bless you, and I rejoice to see you soon.

THE THIRD PENTECOST

Niko Njotorahardjo

These days, I'm reminded of the Lord's prayer. One part of the prayer says, "Your kingdom come." This petition, "Your kingdom come," must be spoken daily, in the same way as we say, "Give us this day our daily bread."

Praying "Your kingdom come," means we are praying for the return of the Lord Jesus, because we long for his coming again. Like the early church always said earnest prayers because of their longing for the Lord's coming, we must keep doing so today. When the disciples asked for the signs of His coming and the end of the age, the Lord Jesus responded with a list of several things, one of which is recorded in Matthew 24:14: "And this gospel of the kingdom will be preached in all the world as a witness to all the nations, and then the end will come."

If you long for His second coming, then clearly you will desire to see the gospel reach all nations as soon as possible. In fact, the Lord Jesus gave us the Great Commission so that we would evangelize and make disciples from all nations. Who is a disciple of the Lord Jesus? According to 1 John 2:6, a disciple is one who lives as Jesus lived, who walks as Jesus walked. When we live as Christ lived, we become a likeness of his image. Our goal as believers is to become a likeness of the image of Jesus. That is, to become a disciple. The Great Commission cannot be completed in our own strength; we have been given the power of the Holy Spirit in order to become witnesses for Christ.

This is why, when Jesus ascended into Heaven, he gave the final message to his disciples, found in Acts 1:8: "But you shall receive power when the Holy Spirit has come upon you and you shall be my witnesses in Jerusalem and all Judea and Samaria and to the end of the earth". After Jesus ascended into Heaven, 120 disciples went to Jerusalem and gathered in the upper room. They did so because the Lord had commanded them not to depart Jerusalem until they were equipped with power from on high. For ten days, they continued with one accord, in prayer and supplication. Then, they gathered on the day of Pentecost. The Holy Spirit came down, and they were filled with Him. The initial evidence of those filled with Holy Spirit is that they spoke in tongues.

They received power to become Jesus' witnesses in order to fulfill the Great Commission. This is what I call the first Pentecost. The first Pentecost was great—why? Because, within approximately one hundred years, seventy percent of the known world, who were living under the Roman Empire, became Christians. Was the Great Commission finished? No, not yet.

In 1906, at Azusa Street in Los Angeles, the Holy Spirit was again pulled out. A servant of the Lord by the name of William Seymour was mightily used by God. This is what I call the second Pentecost. The second Pentecost was great—why? Because according to Gordon Conwell Theological Seminary, 77.9% of Christianity today began in 1900, and the extraordinary outpouring of the Holy Spirit took place in 1906. Today, there are approximately 700 million Pentecostals as a result of the second Pentecost.

Was the great commission complete? No, not yet. In 1909, William Seymour prophesied that in approximately one hundred years, there will be greater Holy Spirit outpouring, which will exceed the outpouring at Azusa Street. This movement would cover the entire world, and would not stop until the return of the Lord Jesus again. In early 2009, the Lord showed to me Revelation 3:11 part a: "Behold, I'm coming quickly." Frequently, I had heard this word before; but this time there was something different. Trembling, I asked the Lord, "What are You going to do, and what must be done?"

The Lord did not immediately answer. Then in the middle of 2009, the Lord spoke to me, "I will pull out my spirit! I will pull out my spirit!" When the Holy Spirit pulls out, it will be like it is written in the book of Joel 2:28-32: There will be three signs that will take place at a time the Holy Spirit pulls out. The first sign is that children, youth, and adults will be mightily used by God. The second sign is that mighty miracles will take place. The third sign is that mighty shakings will happen. As these three signs happen, the fulfillment of verse 32 will also take place. Many will call upon the name of the Lord, and whoever does will be saved. A good harvest will take place. At the end of 2009, I met with Dr. Bill Wilson in Atlanta. At the time, Dr. Bill Wilson asked me to preach and represent Asia at the Global Empowered21 event on the campus of Oral Roberts University, Tulsa, Oklahoma in April 2010.

I asked, "What's Empowered21?" Dr. Wilson gave an explanation, and then I understood that Empowered21 was about what the Holy Spirit would do in the future, and the empowerment of young people. Once in 2006, in Los Angeles, there had been a celebration of the works done by the Holy Spirit during the past one hundred years. Empowered21 was a continuation of this revelation. When I heard the vision of Empowered21, I understood it was the answer concerning what the Lord had spoken to me. I was willing to attend. During this event, my sister Christian, a prayer intercessor, saw a vision in the prayer tower at Oral Roberts University. She saw writing that said, "It's here—it's the year of God's glory." The next day, Dr. Billy Wilson came to me and said that the next Empowered21 Event would be outside of America. And the Lord said it must be in Asia.

I was asked to be the host. I immediately said yes because of that vision. In 2011, the first Empowered21 Asia was held in Indonesia, at the Central International Conference Center. It was attended by delegates from almost 50 nations. As it turns out, that was a trigger for the Empowered21 Movement to follow. In 2013, the second Empowered21 Asia was held at the Central International Conference Center. Two days prior to this event, after I had been processed by the Lord for six months, the Lord spoke to me: "Niko, all this time I've been speaking about the outpouring of the Holy Spirit. That is the third Pentecost." I didn't understand what was meant by the third Pentecost, but the Lord told me that the first Pentecost happened at the upper room in Jerusalem. The second Pentecost happened at Azusa Street in 1906. I believe what the Lord said, even though I did not understand. Like the apostle Paul said, "I believe and therefore I speak."

I began to speak about the third Pentecost during the second Empowered21 Asia Event. As I was declaring the third Pentecost, I received an email from a minister in India. I did not know him. He wrote, "Praise the Lord, Pastor Niko. We are entering a new Pentecost. This is consistent with the 1909 prophecy by William Seymour." It was only then that I knew that William Seymour had prophesied what would happen in these days—the awesome outpouring of the Holy Spirit which exceeds the experiences at Azesa Street. In 2013, I asked the Lord, "What will happen in Indonesia with the third Pentecost?" The Lord did not immediately answer. The Lord answered in 2017 through a vision experienced by Russell Evans of Planetshakers, in Melbourne, Australia.

What did he see about Indonesia? He saw the fire of the Holy Spirit coming down upon Indonesia in a great manner. He saw massive clouds, as if blown out from Indonesia, traveling to the nations. He saw millions of young people blazing in the fire of the Holy Spirit, loving the Lord Jesus with all their hearts and without reservation, who did not compromise to sin. They served the nation of Indonesia as never before. Based on this, I told Dr. Bill Wilson that I would host the third Empowered21 Asia Event in 2018. Dr. Bill Wilson responded, "Whatever you receive from the Lord, I will support."

The Lord said to me, "Invite the nations to come, especially from Asia." The response was great. Two months before the event, the registration had to be closed because we were over capacity. We witnessed delegates from approximately 50 nations.

The fire of the third Pentecost was pulled out by the Lord. Many ministers testified that this event was unlike any other they had ever experienced. I responded, "Yes, they are right, because it is something new. It is the third Pentecost." Cindy Jacobs has prophesied that I would become the messenger of the third Pentecost. She said, "If the second Pentecost, which took place at Azusa Street, spread as a movement from the West to the East, then the third Pentecost movement will spread from the East to the West." Therefore, the meaning of the third Pentecost is as follows.

Firstly, the third Pentecost is a great outpouring of the Holy Spirit—an outpouring which is greater than the one experienced at Azusa Street. Secondly, the third Pentecost will result in the greatest and final harvest of souls before the Lord Jesus comes again. Thirdly, the third Pentecost will raise up the Jeremy generation—this young people filled with the Holy Spirit, who love the Lord Jesus with all of their hearts and without reservation—who do not compromise with sin and who seek to win lost souls. Fourthly, the third Pentecost originated in Indonesia and is moving to the nations. This movement is moving from the East to the West, and back to Jerusalem. Fifthly, the third Pentecost provides the power to finish the Great Commission, and to usher in the return of our Lord Jesus.

What must we do to enter into the era of the third Pentecost? First, according to John chapter 17, the body of Christ must be in unity. Unity is the main key to the great harvest of souls. The second thing we must do was also done during the first Pentecost and the second Pentecost: they continued in prayer, praise, and worship to maintain that unity, day and night. This is also the key to the restoration of the Tabernacle of David.

The Lord has prepared our church for more than 30 years with the restoration of the tabernacle of David as our church DNA. We hadn't been told that this was preparation to enter the era of the third Pentecost. The third Pentecost Movement is beginning to spread to the other nations, and I believe that what the Lord has said concerning the meaning of the third Pentecost will be fulfilled throughout the whole world.

INNOVATION AND DISRUPTION

Rob Hoskins

I want to take this opportunity to share why I am so excited about Jerusalem2020, this global gathering of the Spirit-empowered community coming from every corner of the earth. What excites me is not just the fact that we are coming together for the sake of unity, but that we're coming together for the sake of a mission. The mission of Empowered21 is simple: that every person on earth would have an authentic encounter with Jesus Christ through the power and presence of the Holy Spirit by Pentecost 2033. That's a massive undertaking.

I remember when I was just a young man in my 20s, and the Soviet Union was beginning to break up. I was actually on a flight from Vladivostok, which was in the far east corner of the Soviet Union, flying to Moscow. This was about an 11-hour flight. While I was on that flight, they had an unscheduled stop in a city called Ulaanbaatar. I became very excited. Ulaanbaatar was in the country of Mongolia. Ever since I was a young child, as the son of a missionary, I had prayed with my parents about the uttermost parts of the earth. To me, Ulaanbaatar was the outermost parts of the earth. Here I was, stopping in Mongolia. At the time, no Americans were allowed to be in the country. I thought, "I'm going to be one of the first, if not the only American ever to step foot in Mongolia."

ABLAZE—A PROPHETIC CALL TO IGNITE THE CHURCH

The plane stopped. Sadly, they announced that, as an American, I wasn't allowed to get off the plane. They were going to just on-board some passengers from Mongolia that were going to Moscow with us. I became excited again—I was going to see Mongolians for the first time. The longer I sat there on that hot tarmac, the more I began to think about what they would look like. I was expecting some big furs, big hats, and piercings. Instead, a group of Mongolian university students on their way to study at Moscow University got on the plane.

Most of them were wearing Levi blue jeans. They had on all different types of t-shirts with logos. One had an ACDC t-shirt on. Many of them had a Walkman in their possession. As I listened in, they were listening to Madonna and Michael Jackson at the time (this was in the late eighties). Four of them sat in my row—between the four of them, they spoke seven languages. It was startling to me. They knew who Michael Jackson was, they knew who Madonna was, they knew Michael Jordan was, but they had no idea who Christ, the Son of God, was.

We still live in a world where 82% of all Muslims, Buddhists, Hindus, and animists have never once had a personal encounter with Jesus Christ. When we talk about the mandate and the mission of Empowered21—that every person on earth would have an authentic encounter with Jesus Christ through the power and presence of the Holy spirit by Pentecost 2033—we realize that we still have a massive undertaking in the places in this world where the name of Jesus is not yet known. I have to tell you, since the late eighties and early nineties, things have not slowed down with this global youth culture that has been impacted by media.

We are in the midst of a digital transformation that is disrupting our world in unprecedented ways. The world is speeding up. It's sped up through the dynamics of globalization, connectivity, and urbanization powered by the digital revolution. All of this has accelerated change at a mind-numbing pace; and it's actually changing everything. In the short time we have, we can't fully explore the dynamics of the Kairos moment of change we're now living in; but this change will affect every inch of our planet.

Some might say, "Well this is a phenomenon of the Western, developing world." No, it's actually something that's covering the entire world. Let's take Africa for example, which already has 80% mobile penetration and 36% internet penetration. The digital transformation is shifting the lives of millennials. 60% of all young people in Africa now have social media as their primary source of information; 46% of young people are active in one to three WhatsApp groups daily. The smartphone phenomenon has taken over the lives of young people all over the world: Africa, Asia, and Latin America.

In some ways, it's like a Trojan horse, because inside of the digital revolution and its mechanisms, there come the values of individualism, materialism, secularism, and pluralism. We have experienced, in the West alone, in less than one generation, a complete reversal of the values around identity and sexual orientation. If any of you feel that where you live is immune to this spirit of the age, then you need to wake up. But it's not just a new reality around technology and innovation; it's actually disrupting our very ideas and our beliefs and our values.

It's interesting for us to say that disruption and innovation is something new to the kingdom of God, because disruption has always been happening. In fact, it happened at the very beginning. When we think about the creation story in Genesis, there are actually two creation stories there. There's God's creation of the world; but there's also man's creation. We see this in the life of Cain, who kills his brother Abel. God comes to him and says, "Cain, because of your sin, you're going to be condemned to be a wanderer on the earth. This is the repercussions of your sin."

Cain actually protests: "God, this penalty is too severe." He's saying, "I don't deserve this," when actually what he really deserves is death. Out of love, God says, "I'm going to put a mark of protection on you, Cain, so that no one can kill you, even though you're a wanderer."

Cain, in that moment, rejects the protection of God, rejects the destiny that God has provided for his life. The Word says that he goes East of Eden and builds a city called Enoch. Cain's response, man's response, to God's destiny and plan is to build new innovations and technologies. In this case, Cain builds a city called Enoch. The Hebrew word for Enoch is actually *initiation*. You see, this is the spirit of innovation that is born in every man to innovate, to change, to grow but also to create one's own destiny. This continues in Cain's family with Nimrod, who is the father of many kingdoms and civilizations.

Each of the cities listed in Genesis that Nimrod built actually have unique qualities about them: technology and information and education. This results in the ultimate city that man builds, which is the city of Babel—which Nimrod also built. We know the story of Babel. It's is an attempt by man to throw off God's destiny for his life and build his own destiny. As it says, they went to Babel "to make a name for themselves." And so they build Babel, which becomes Babylon, which becomes the spirit of the age.

This is the spirit of innovation that has always existed in man that is in Genesis; this is the story of Cain. Man has always been initiating. Ever since Cain's rejection of God's destiny over his life, the world has been disruptive. It continues today through the development of new technologies. It's critical for us to understand that we are living in a very disruptive world; but it's also important for us to understand how God responds to man's spirit of initiation to innovation. Why? Because it's important for us to know how to respond to this digital age, and to mirror God's response.

You see, God never disengages from man's initiative. He's working throughout history for our own good. We find this in the story of Israel: Israel defied God's plan for their life. They fell into sin again and again. Because of their sin, Israel and Judah and Jerusalem, the city of God that we will visit for Jerusalem2020, have become places of utter destruction. They have been destroyed, and Babylon has taken the children of Israel captive. It seems like the story of Israel, and God's people, is over.

What is God's startling response to man's rejection? You would think it would be condemnation, rejection. Instead, in Jeremiah 29, we find one of our favorite passages of Scripture in the entire Bible. It says that God has come to give us a hope and a future. In many ways, we misapply that Scripture more deeply than any other Scripture in the Word. In context, that Scripture is delivered to the Jews living as captives in the subcultural, suburban slums of Babylon.

The prophet Jeremiah is declaring to them that, instead of rebelling and standing in opposition to the city, the children of God should move into the heart of the city. Their hope and their future is found there; as the city prospers, so shall they. You see, their temporary captivity results in a hope and a future found within man's city of disruptive innovation.

We see the loving and merciful character of God here. He will redeem what we have built in defiance. He will restore what has been initiated in rebellion, and He will reform what has been twisted for evil. He builds us a city. He started us out in a garden, and we rejected him through our sin; but He accepts our initiation and our vision of a city, and He will take our initiative and make it perfect.

You see, at the end of time, the end of this world will come by the return of Jesus and the coming down of a city—a new heaven and earth. We started in a garden, but our future ends in a city. This is God's redemptive power. He has initiated his kingdom, and this kingdom is the here and now. Instead of us simply saying, "Well, what man initiated—this digital revolution—is just causing rampant sin and rebellion," I think the same word comes to us today as it came to the children of Israel, living in Babylon: move into the city; move into the technology; move into the disruption.

Through the power of the Holy Spirit, we have the capability of reforming it, of renewing it, of restoring in it God's intentional purposes for his people. As God's people, we are constantly having to do what God himself did, which was to restore what has been broken. The church is in a constant state of disruption because the world is in a constant state of disruption. I love what Hans Kung said: "The church cannot do without the constant renewal of its form." Renewal of form implies a change of form by means of human decision and responsibility.

Changing times demand changing forms. You see, the church has an enormous task, both familiar and unfamiliar, that confronts us. We must see ourselves as a part of this change in the world. How do we do that? As the Spirit-empowered community, we believe God has uniquely provided power for us through the gifts of the Holy Spirit, in order to bring about dynamic change and reformation in this world.

The book of Acts is a living chronology of innovation and disruption. As soon as the church begins to settle into their comfort, Stephen is murdered. Phillip is transported. Saul is blinded. Peter has a vision. And Cornelius, the Gentile, disrupts the happy Jews in their present state. The church is constantly, including in its earliest forms, being disrupted by the Holy Spirit, so that they know what to do at the right moment, according to the wisdom and knowledge of God. Through the Holy Spirit moving in the hearts of men and women, things began to happen.

Letters are written by Paul, in prison, that reform the church. The Roman roads exist so that the gospel can travel further and faster than it ever has before. Shipwrecks and jailings provide us with the Word of God that guides us today. The kingdom is in a constant state of disruption and innovation; and when we lose our way, God will shake the world again. We find this throughout church history. We find it with the Gutenberg Press coming onto the scenes, making the Word of God available to the common people. Another reformation happens in the church, which comes out of its darkness and lethargy.

Engaging with the Scripture in new, fresh ways in our world results in new great awakenings—all of which use, rather than despise, innovation and technology. I lead a ministry that my parents built on the power of the printed page. It's called OneHope. Our mission is God's Word, every child. We began to wonder as a ministry, "What does it look like in the 21st century to engage this next generation with God's Word?" Imagine it. Being in a ministry sphere that has been so consumed with print for nearly 30 years, we thought, "What would it look like for children to engage with Scripture on a mobile device?"

We prayed that the Holy Spirit would speak to us. He began to lead us through the gifts of the Holy Spirit. We designed what became the Bible App for Kids. Through that innovation, children from zero to six years old could now engage with Scripture in a fresh, new way on their mobile device, through gamification, audio content, and visual content.

Since that app was launched, 35 million children around the world have downloaded it and are engaging with the Scripture in a new way. We have to be innovative. We have to continually be asking ourselves, "How do we take all that God's given us and allow the Holy Spirit to infuse that into our lives?" I think of my friend Mart Green, who will be with us at Jerusalem2020, along with Bobby Grunewald from YouVersion and so many of the other great innovators God has been using—men and women who are filled with the Holy Spirit.

Several years ago, we were praying, and the Holy Spirit was speaking to us. We determined that we needed a new Bible translation revolution to take place. If we continued in our present pace, it would take until the year 2150, nearly 150 years, for the Bible Project to be started in every language. Mart Green and his team started a new Bible course, called Every Tribe Every Nation (ETEN). This program was designed to use innovation and collaboration in a new way.

The good news is that by 2033, a Bible translation project will be started in every language of the world. We live in a new, unique time—this age of globalization—but we need to fully leverage the power of the Holy Spirit. We can't be bound by tradition. Jaroslav Pelikan has said it this way: "Tradition is the living faith of the dead, but traditionalism is the dead faith of the living."

E21, we need to celebrate our rich past; but we also need to be praying that the power of the Holy Spirit, as it says in Acts 2:17, will come upon us in these last days—that the Spirit of God would be poured out upon all flesh, so that our sons and our daughters should prophesy, so that young men shall see visions, and so that old men will dream dreams. That's what I'm praying for Jerusalem2020.

As we gather together the best minds, the best leaders, of the Spirit-empowered community from around the world, I'm praying that a fresh new wave of the Holy Spirit would fall upon us. I pray that we would build a platform for Empowered21 to do what we say we will do—to address the crucial issues facing the 21st century Spirit-empowered church, and to discover the contemporary methods, vocabulary, spiritual grace, and relational favor needed to engage every generation in Spirit-empowered living.

I pray that we would witness greater convergence and collaboration of the Holy Spirit-empowered ministries around the world. We're going to be doing that in Jerusalem. And I pray for unity—that we would have strategic leadership that empowers us to build something the world has never seen—something to address the grave concerns in the world, so that the world can be transformed through the power of the Holy Spirit.

Join us in Jerusalem2020 as we think and pray about this mission being accomplished in fresh, new, imaginative ways.

ABLAZE—A PROPHETIC CALL TO IGNITE THE CHURCH

Join us as God's people meet the Holy Spirit in an upper room and are transformed by Him to meet the needs of our generation. I hope you're there. I can't wait to see you. God bless you.

THE SOUND BARRIER

Russell Evans

I looked up what happens when the sound barrier is broken. The sound barrier is broken when an object travels faster than the speed of sound. This is what I feel God's about to do.

Something moving faster than the sound that's released from it…think about that. We often talk about our words forming our worlds, and that's true. The Bible says that there is life and death in the power of the tongue. God spoke the world into existence. Everything comes through sound. But sound needs to produce something.

Faith without works is dead. I believe, prophetically, that we are stepping into a season in which our actions, and the momentum of our actions, is going to surpass our declarations. That's breaking the sound barrier. You see, our sound of praise propels us into another sphere, another level. That's why we need to be a praising church. When our sound comes together, it releases a whole new atmosphere over our life, so that we can never afford to stop praising.

In fact, praise is what actually opens a door to heaven. You say, "What do you mean?" The Bible says, "Enter his courts with thanksgiving." So I come with praise into His courts. My praise sets me up. The Lord's Prayer starts with, "Our Father."

Why? Because it's praise—it's talking about how great He is. Our sound of praise propels us.

On the other hand, a sound of criticism drags us down. When we listen to criticism and negativity, it slows us. The enemy tries to counter our sounds of praise by bringing criticism, unbelief, and disunity. He might say, "This is happening!" so that we get caught up in the circumstances, instead of responding, "No, this is what God says about my life. This is what God says about my family. This is what God says about my city."

You see, every sound that God releases, the enemy tries to release a counter sound to slow you down. We are Planetshakers; we are praisers; we are encouragers. We don't live in a cynical, critical mindset. We live in a positive, faith-filled mindset. The sound of faith overcomes the sound of fear. A sound of faith is an antidote to the fear that tries to drag on me. When our praise sounds are going out—our prayer sounds, our worship sounds, our faith declaration sounds—it creates momentum.

Ephesians 3:20 says, "Now to Him by (in consequence of) the action of His power that is at work within us is able to carry out His purpose..." What's His purpose? " . . . to do super abundantly, far over and above all we dare ask or think (infinitely beyond our highest prayers, thoughts, or hopes, hopes or dreams)." So what is this saying? God wants to bring superabundance that will surpass our sounds of asking, our sounds of praying. I believe God's going to release us into a momentum in our actions that is way ahead of our declarations. Think about that. That's called warp speed.

When you're in such momentum that things are happening before you even declare them—favor's happening; blessing's happening; healing's happening; salvation is happening; miracles are happening—the sounds are being released, but now superabundance takes over.

It says, "Infinitely beyond our highest prayers, desires, thoughts, hopes, or dreams." I want to give you six quick points on this passage. Let's explore it more deeply together.

KINGDOM DECLARATIONS POINT US IN THE RIGHT DIRECTION.

If you are declaring negativity, you're pointing to problems. If you're declaring promises, you're pointing to momentum. We're to be people who continue to make kingdom declarations—people who declare the goodness of God. We are people that declare the favor of God, even in challenging times. We don't get caught up with challenges. We get caught up with the potential and the purposes of God. We deal with the challenges, but we focus on the promise.

What are you declaring over your life? What are you declaring over your family and friends? What are your declaring over volunteers? What are you declaring over your finances? What are you declaring?

Praise and thanksgiving start the engine of faith. So I declare, and now I praise God for what I'm declaring. "God, we're going to see the city well. I thank you God for this city being well. I declare financial blessings. I thank you for your financial blessings. I declare freedom and liberty. I thank you for freedom and liberty. I declare that there'll be an increase beyond measure. I thank you for an increase. I give you praise." It starts the engine of faith. When I don't believe, I have to declare and praise, because that starts me believing. Then, agreement and unity propel us. So a kingdom declaration points us in the right direction. Praise and thanksgiving start the engine of faith, and agreement and unity propels us.

I was in a church a little while ago, and they asked me to speak to their staff because I preached there on the Sunday. This church had settled; it wasn't growing. It had good praise and worship, good leadership, good teaching…but it wasn't growing. And I said, "God, it's got all the right ingredients, but why isn't it growing?" And this is what He said to me: "They have a level of unity, but there's a deeper level. They love the vision of the pastor, but they don't love each other enough." And so I got up in front of the staff and I said, "You want to know the problem? You're not growing." And they're like, "What?" I said, "Do you know why you're not growing? Because you're not unified enough. You have this department, which likes its own self, and this department, which likes its own self, and this department, which likes their own self, instead of each department loving each other and loving the vision of the church together."

See, unity is what commands a blessing. If God wants to take us into warp speed, unity is the fuel that gets God to say, "Go for it." That's why at times, God in His genius, says, "You know what? There are some people I need to get out for a little while, because they're not in unity. They're stopping the flow."

We have to be in such a flow with one another, and the vision to which God's taking us—in flow with God—that we're all walking together. Jesus put it so awesomely when someone asked Him, "What is the greatest commandment?" He said, "Love the Lord your God with all your heart and love others as yourself." What does this mean? Be in unity with God; and as you are in unity with God, you'll be in unity with other people.

Declaration points us to where we're going. Praise and worship starts the engine of faith. Agreement and unity is what is propelling us, commanding a blessing. Then, actions of faith keep the momentum going. It's good to declare; it's good to thank.

I remember praying, "God send revival," and He said, "Okay." I said, "Would you go and touch a city?" He says "Go on then." And I said, "No, no, You do it." He goes, "Yeah, I will—through you. You're praying for the miracle that you carry." Faith without works is dead. The Bible says, "How will they know unless somebody tells them?" The Bible never says to pray for the harvest. It doesn't say, "Pray for the harvest," even though it's okay to do so. The Bible says, "Pray for the workers, for the harvest is plentiful, but the laborers are few."

The key to a harvest is laborers going out. It amazes me at times that people say, "I just want to go to a small church where you can know everybody. I just want to be in a family church." Why can't you have a big church that has family?

See, if I'm going to a small church so I can get to know everybody, I'm a selfish Christian. If I really love the city, I want every church to be massive, and huge, and powering on. God wants to fill the churches with people. Actions of faith keep the momentum going. I believe with all my heart, because I felt God speak to me about this, that Planetshakers we will be a supernatural church always—miracles, signs, wonders, breakthroughs, healings, life, joy, peace, heaven on earth. That's what we're about. But I also believe we will be the hands and feet of Jesus.

My goal is that, within the next five or ten years, we become the biggest givers to charity in the city of Melbourne.

Whether that's in volunteers, building hires, money, support… anything. I really believe that we could feed 2,000 families every week. We're going to roll it out. We're going to put action behind it. We're going to go and do it. We're going to change the world. God's setting it up.

Action keeps the momentum going. A church that only worships, but doesn't do, is also selfish. It amazes me how many churches don't do salvation altar calls. If I go out fishing, and there's fish there, I want to throw my line in the water and get some fish. But if I don't put the line out, the fish will never bite, and I'll miss the opportunity to connect with them. The most depth—the most joy— you can have as a Christian is to see people saved. So let's be action people with our money. Let's be action people with our volunteer time. Let's be action people with who we're looking to share the love of Jesus with. Let's be action people.

Okay, so we're in action. We have this momentum going…and then there's a bit of turbulence. There's a bit of drag. What do we do now? You've got to get rid of anything that'll put a drag on your momentum. Some of us, at times, allow other people to put a drag on our momentum. And don't get me wrong—we're to love everybody; but there's a time to say, "Hey, we're going there. We love you. We want you to come with us. But we're going there, whether you're coming or not." We've got to get rid of any lies that the enemy's told about us about others—get rid of them.

This is how I started. I'm here to tell you, because I feel that God is saying this so strongly, that we're going to get to a place where our actions pass our sounds. We'll go, "God, give us two-fifty. . ." Oh, we have 300 saved. "God, we're believing for $200. . ." We got half a million in offerings. "Oh, God, we want to feed two. . ." We're feeding 3000. "Oh, God, we want to see this amount of small groups." Wait, what? Wow. "God, we want to pay off our. . ." We've paid off other people's debts. Oh, wow. "God, we need a building there." It's there.

There will be a moment in which our actions will pass our declaration, our sound. How? We declared it, and He did super abundantly far over and above all we dared ask.

So what are you declaring over 2020? I'm so excited for this year. I'm getting on board. I'm going to get my declaration, and I'm going to speak it. I'm going to come with thanksgiving. I'm going to come with praise.

BE HOLY, BE ONE, BE LIGHT

Samuel Rodriguez

If I hear anything resonating from the heart of God, by the leading of the Holy Spirit, regarding 2020, it's be holy, be one, and be light.

I know everyone's focusing on vision and its application for 2020. I sense an admonition, a clarion call, from heaven for the church to be holy. And by "holy," I don't mean in a legalistic sense. I mean embracing the grace-filled work of Jesus—a position from which we pursue righteousness, live above reproach, and live in accordance and adherence to God's Word. This is the holiness we're called to as believers.

This idea of grace-filled, faith-substantiated, holiness or integrity doesn't spring from what we do. We are holy because of Him who occupies our lives. We are holy because of the Holy Spirit.

First Peter 1:16 says: "Be holy for I am holy." This is a clarion call from heaven: "Be holy; walk like me; talk like me; think like me; live like me; forgive like me; preach like me; heal like me, change the world like I changed the world." John 14:12 says that we will do the greater things that were promised. How? Be holy. That's the call.

Not only are we called to be holy, but we are called to be one. John 17:21 says, "That they all may all be one, just as you, Father, are in me, and I in you, that they may also be in us, so that the world may believe that you have sent me." This prayer of Jesus really speaks to each and every one of us. What if the church comes together?

I am so frustrated with the notion of a fragmented, hyphenate church. There is no such animal as a black church, a white church, a yellow church, a brown church. There's only one church: the church of Jesus Christ. And the church can come together around the centrality of Christ, committed to biblical orthodoxy, the Word of God. We can change the world. A divided church can never heal a broken nation or a broken world. But a united church can change the world. God is saying to his church, "Be one, come together. Stop fighting about the minutia. Stop focusing on the differences, but become one, be one."

If we are holy, and we are one, then we can be light.

Matthew 5:14-16 is a passage I've preached on and written a book on. It's a call to turn on the light, rather than focusing on the darkness around us. Let's look at it together:

"You are the light of the world. A city set on a hill cannot be hidden. Nor do people light a lamp and put it under a basket, but on a stand, and it gives light to all in the house. In the same way, let your light shine before others, so that they may see your good works and give glory to your Father who is in heaven."

This light—the light of Christ in us—always wins—every single time it stands next to darkness. I believe we stand at the precipice of a fresh move of God's Holy Spirit. It's a Holy Spirit move that will usher in a fresh, 21st century holiness movement. Again, this will be a grace-substantiated holiness movement.

The second thing it will usher in is a call to unity, and third, the call to be light. We're going to reach the next generation. I live in the state of California. California, spiritually speaking, is known for what took place in Azusa—the Jesus movement. We are known even for what's currently taking place in Redding, California—a beautiful movement through a network of churches led by Bethel, Jesus Culture, and other churches who are experiencing beautiful, unprecedented moves of God. I believe California will again experience a fresh outpouring of God's Holy Spirit that will impact America and, subsequently, the world. It's a multi-generational, multi-ethnic, Christ-centered, Bible-based, Spirit-empowered movement. We are at the precipice of a fresh Pentecost, but it requires us to be holy, to be one, and to be light.

That's what I feel the Holy Spirit is placing right now upon the church. That will open up our eyes to 2020 vision. What's that vision? When we're holy, when we're one, when we're light, I believe we're about to see what we've never seen before: an unbridled, unprecedented move of God's Holy Spirit. Then we can articulate the words of the apostle Paul: "Be imitators of me as I am of Christ."

The hashtag would be, #WatchMe. Watch me glorify and magnify Jesus like I've never glorified and magnified Jesus before. Watch us exhibit the glory of God. Watch us preach the gospel in and out of season. Watch us make disciples, equip the saints, and worship God in spirit and truth. Watch us do justice, love mercy, and walk humbly before God. Watch us quench the thirst, feed the hungry, welcome the stranger, bring good news to the poor, freedom to the captive, healing to the brokenhearted. Watch us declare the favor of God upon every single person who embraces the good news of the gospel. Watch us exhibit the majesty of Jesus' broken world.

Be holy, be one, be light. That's what's next. And if we do all of this in the name of Jesus, for the glory of God, I do believe we will see Christians filled with the Holy Spirit, living holy, healed, healthy, happy, humble, hungry, honoring lives. And with these lives, we will do nothing less than change the world. That's what I believe the Holy Spirit is saying to his church. Let's do this.

A HOLISTIC REVIVAL

Stovall Weems

What is God doing, and where is the church headed in 2020? Well, I believe that in 2020, we're not only entering into a new season—we're entering into a new time. You know, in Acts 3, the Scripture says that Jesus must remain in heaven until the restoration of all things. I really think that, prophetically and scripturally, we're moving from a time from revival to a time of restoration. In other words, we've experienced great revivals in the past. We've filled stadiums. We had great events. We've seen God do some amazing things through some amazing men and women, churches and ministries. These past fifty years have been amazing.

But now, I believe the Lord is heading in a direction that includes the big event. It includes the preaching of the gospel, but it's a much more holistic view of what revival is really for. The Lord is moving us into understanding what it means to become a people. To do that, we have to answer the question, "What is the church?" Our mentality has shifted to a place where we regard church (and revival) in terms of the building, the services, the events. But if we really look into what the Bible says in Acts and the epistles about the *ecclesia*, the called out ones, we see that the churches is three-fold. The church is the people of God. It is the priesthood of all believers. It is the family of God. And that manifests in three ways.

First, there's the home. All of the apostle Paul's churches were in homes—most of them were gatherings of about 30-40 people. Rome was a little bit bigger. The core of the church is the home.

Then, there's what we call the building, or the synagogue. That's where the community comes in and hears the word of God. It has a different dynamic. I would say that this is the local church now. This aspect is crucial, because it's through the local church that we equip God's people to do the work of the ministry. There's also the regional church. Think of Jesus's letters to the churches in Revelation. Those were regional churches. So what I see is a move of God that brings restoration and wholeness to the home, the family. It also brings restoration, or wholeness, to the local church, in the way of equipping the priesthood of believers to do the work of the ministry. Then, it brings wholeness to the regional church.

This is a revival that brings restoration reformation. It's not just a two-hour event with a big speaker or a big worship team. It's so much more holistic than that—it will equip us for the hundreds of hours outside of that event. If we don't take the home back—if we don't take the family back—what does it matter if we can get people to church? If God touches them and heals them, but their homes are in chaos because they're not equipped or empowered to lead their families and be a light in their neighborhoods, they'll still be at a severe disadvantage.

So Scripturally, what we see is a need to come into agreement—to come to an understanding that it takes all of us in a region. Kingdom authority has nothing to do with your church size. Look at the apostle Paul—his churches were small by today's standard. Does that mean Paul had less authority than someone with a bigger church? No, just the opposite. I would say that kingdom authority is the lessening of ourselves.

Jesus said, "The Son of Man did not come to be served, but to serve, and to give his life as a ransom for many." What He was saying is that, in God's kingdom, there's authority; but there's not hierarchy. We are all equals. It's a kingdom of priests. That's God's dream team. Where I see things headed now is toward a cohesive effort of the home church, the local church, and the regional church coming together. That's what I love about Jerusalem2020 being on the feast day of Pentecost. I know that many of us will be traveling there from all over the world; but the key is those Jerusalem pastors in that region—they hold the authority. If God's going to bring revival to Israel, he's doing it through the church. So our part is helping to support those pastors as they come together.

The regional revival is meant to empower the family to do the work of the ministry. I'm a pastor of a local church. Imagine if you came to me and said, "Hey, are you a pastor?" I would say, "Yes." If you ask me, "Okay, when are your services?" I would say, "Well, we don't have any services. There's no gathering of our church family where we take communion and declare the word of the Lord." If I said that to them, they would be like, "Well, you're not really pastoring people. You're not really feeding God's sheep."

I would say the same thing about the priesthood of the believer. Let's take the example of a husband and wife in their home. If they're leading their family in the presence of God, just like we do in the local congregation, they don't have a service of their own. That's why I'm a big believer in the Lord's table—communion—in the home once a week. If they're single, they can get together with family or friends. But there has to be dominion and demonstration in the homes, in the community centers, in the neighborhoods, where we can be the city—the light on the hill.

That's not talking about the building. Revival has to be holistic. We have an Awakening event every January, where we'll have 8,000 people gathered; people get saved, people are healed, and all those other things we love. But what happens the other 364 nights out of the year? How is that sustained?

I'd rather have those 8,000 people praying and seeking God, serving communion to their family and friends, and praying for revival and restoration and healing every single week. But thing about that is, it's not visible. You can't take pictures of it. It doesn't work on Instagram. And so I encourage all of us who are passionate for a move of God, and the glory of God, to seek a holistic form of revival that brings restoration into the home and the family. It doesn't have to be sustained by the man of God in the pulpit; it is sustained, and grows like wildfire, in the people.

Let's make sure that we have different influences in our social circles. Let's make sure that we at least have a few pastors in our region with whom we can come into agreement. Let's make sure that we're not just relating to people according to their church size, thinking that makes those pastors of smaller churches less valuable for revival in the kingdom of God. Let's understand that every person that the Lord sends to our region He sends for a purpose. The more people we can get in agreement, repenting to one another, forgiving one another, interceding for our region, interceding for our community, the better.

We're going to start seeing some real breakthroughs in the unity of churches in different regions. Many regions are way ahead in this regard. We have to focus on the priesthood of the believer, and taking back the home—empowering believers to declare the Word of God and pray for their local communities. Then, the local church will be seen as a body that truly equips its people.

Ephesians 4 says, "Until we all come into unity of the faith." There are not enough buildings, preachers, or church staff to make this happen on their own. Just think about it; run the numbers. How limited are we if we can be contained in a stadium, listening to one anointed preacher? We're all anointed! I love all the great anointed preachers and teachers; but if we're going to see a real move of God that is brings both restoration and reformation, we're going to have to look at it a different way. We're going to need a more holistic way of the *ecclesia* in order to see God's heaven come to our earth.

We're going to see the glory of the Lord cover the earth by 2033. That means we've got a job to do. Let's get to work.

THE WORLD THROUGH FOUR LENSES

Todd Johnson

My name is Todd Johnson, and I'm co-director of the Center for the Study of Global Christianity at Gordon-Conwell Theological Seminary in South Hamilton, Massachusetts.

Now, I've been here for about 16 or 17 years; but our research has been going on for the last 54 years. We started in 1965 in Nairobi, Kenya, and we've been in continuous operation ever since. What we do is we study Christianity all around the world—every kind of Christian group, every single country—and we try to understand what's happening in global Christianity. We've been working the past five years on a special project called the World Christian Encyclopedia. It's our third edition, and we've learned a lot about what's happening all over the world.

What I'd like to do is take you on a quick trip around the world through four different lenses: the lens of Christianity, the lens of Pentecostalism, the lens of other religions, and the lens of Christian mission. I'll try to give you some of the most notable findings of the last five years, in anticipation of us being together in Jerusalem, where I'll show you some amazing charts, graphs, maps, and photos to back all of this up.

ABLAZE—A PROPHETIC CALL TO IGNITE THE CHURCH

The first thing is this: studying Christianity, in one sense, is not very exciting. Over the last hundred years, Christians have made up about a third of the world's population. It almost looks like a flat line, but that actually hides lots of changes in Christianity. Now, when I speak of Christianity, I'm talking about every form of Christianity. We're familiar with the biggest traditions within Christianity, such as Catholicism, Orthodoxy, the Protestant churches, and the independent churches.

But there have also been shifts within the third of the world that practices Christianity. If you live in the Western world, you know that Christians have been declining as a percentage in most Western countries. But if you live in the global South, you know that Christianity has been growing rapidly over the last hundred years. Let me give you just a couple of examples. Africa was only about 9% Christian in 1900. Now, it is about 49% Christian. That's an amazing transformation over about 120 years. Asia has grown from about 2% Christian in 1900 all the way up to about 8%. Christianity is still a minority religion there, but we've seen significant growth nonetheless in places like China, India, and so on.

Now, if we look at this shift specifically in relation to the global South—Africa, Asia, Latin America, and Oceania—only 18% of all Christians were in the global South around the year 1900. Today, in 2020, 67% of all Christians are in the global South. That's two-thirds. That's a huge shift!

One of the other things that's shifting are people's ideas about what Christianity is really like. A lot of people think of Christianity as a Western religion, but when two-thirds of your people are in Africa, Asia, Latin America, and Oceania, you're not a Western religion. That's something we have to make sure people know. The other hidden treasure in this is, if we look back to the first thousand years of Christianity, we find that all the way through the middle of the 10th century, Asians and Africans outnumbered Europeans within our global faith. That's a little surprising because, when people recount the history of Christianity, they often emphasize Europe, Europe, Europe. In actuality, Asia and Africa played a very important role in the early history of Christianity as well. So now, we're back in a position where the vast majority of Christians are from the global South.

Africa is a really special place to think about in relation to this. In 1900, only 1.7% of all Christians in the world were Africans. Today, that figure is 39%. In one sense, we're not a Western religion—we're becoming an African religion. In fact, we're almost at the point where 50% of all Protestant Christians are Africans.

I was staying with a few Africans in Wittenberg, Germany in 2017, and we were talking about the 500th anniversary of the Protestant Reformation. It was interesting because, from the front of this meeting of evangelicals and Pentecostals from around the world, someone said, "Africans are welcome at the table here at this global meeting." I had an African leader at my table, and he leaned over to me and he said, "In my country, we have a proverb: it's good for you to invite me to the table, but it's better if you invite me into the kitchen." That's the challenge for global Christianity. Global Christianity is not a Western religion that invites Africans to the table. We are a global religion, and we need Africans in the kitchen—particularly if they're almost half of all Protestants. This is something we really have to think about.

ABLAZE—A PROPHETIC CALL TO IGNITE THE CHURCH

Now, this story is not all about growth. There are some significant declines within Christianity within this same hundred-year period. I think most of you know that Christianity in the Middle East has been under a lot of pressure over the last century. If we look at the statistics, about 13% of everyone in the Middle East in 1900 was a Christian; that figure is now under 4%. That's a tremendous drop. Think of a country like Turkey. Turkey was 25% Christian in 1900. Today, Turkey is 0.3% Christian. There has been an Exodus of Christians from the Middle East. The sad thing is, as they've been driven out by genocide, war and other factors, Western Christians have been largely silent. That's something that obviously needs to change as we move forward. We want to see Christians located in the place where our faith got started—we want them to be protected and to grow into a vibrant community.

Another challenge we face is that there are now 45,000 Christian denominations in the world. That's right—45,000. These are groups that split off for all sorts of different reasons, such as doctrine, and practices in church and worship. In Korea alone, for example, there are over 200 Presbyterian denominations.

Now, some of this is good, because we have many flavors and varieties of Christianity; different people are attracted to different kinds. Still, we have far too many splits, which is something we have to consider as we continue to preach the gospel. To people who've never heard the good news, they can be a little surprised about how divided we are. It truly weakens our witness as we go forth into the world.

Another problem that we face is that 6.5% of all the money we collect in offerings and through other means is actually stolen from the churches through embezzlement, schemes, fraud, the like. This happens to all kinds of organizations; the church isn't immune. A lot of this money is never recovered. We need a lot more accountability when it comes to finances. That's a challenge for us. Not to mention that we have the prosperity gospel, where different preachers come forward around the world and tell people they need to give a lot of money in order to get money. There have been a lot of problems with finances and fraud in that aspect, as well.

Now, let's take a look at what's happening in global Pentecostalism. There has been tremendous growth over the last 120 years. There used to be less than a million Pentecostal charismatics—what we're now calling Spirit-empowered Christians. We think that there are 644 million in the world today. It's really on the way to a billion. We'll tell you more about this in Jerusalem, but there are three major groups under this. Let's take a look at each one individually.

The first group is the classical Pentecostals. This group is actually the smallest of the three, even though we're talking about 124 million people. The second type are charismatics in mainline churches, including Catholic charismatics, which are the largest portion of this. This group numbers about 252 million. Then finally, there are the independent charismatics, African independent churches, Chinese house churches, and white-led movements of independent charismatics all around the world. They make up about 268 million. These are the major parts of the global Spirit-empowered Christian movement, and it's really remarkable what's happened in the last 120 years.

Now, why do we think that Spirit-empowered Christians are going to grow to a billion in number? There is a lot of evidence for this. Over the past 120 years, numbers of Spirit-empowered Christians grew four times faster than the world's population *and* the Christian population in general. We see it growing perhaps twice as quickly, and that's projected to continue into the next 30 years or so. We expect Spirit-empowered Christians to grow from about a quarter of all Christians in the world to 30% of all Christians in the next 30 years.

Brazil, Colombia, and Argentina—even Mexico—are all places where Spirit-empowered Christianity has grown rapidly over the last 50 years. In Africa we have Nigeria, the Democratic Republic of Congo, South Africa, and Kenya. All over Africa, we see growing numbers of Spirit-empowered Christians.

Now over the last 120 years, we've had Spirit-empowered Christians growing in Oceania and Asia; however, because of high birth rates, we think Africa is going to continue to have one of the fastest-growing sects of Spirit-empowered Christianity. People are converting, and they're having large families, as well. So that's the Pentecostal lens.

Let's talk about religion for a minute. Some of this information is going to seem counterintuitive—it's not what you'd expect. Firstly, the world as a whole is becoming a more religious place every day. Those who live in the West look outside and see signs of secularization. That's a real thing. But in the global South, we see Christianity and other religions growing.

Back in 1970, about 81% of the world's population was religious. Today, it's about 90%, and it's continuing to grow. What's the reason for this? There were so many nonreligious people in 1970 because of communism. The collapse of communism is one major reason why the world is more religious now than it was in 1970. The other factor is the rapid growth of religion in China and India. People are also moving around like never before. There are around 220 million people on the move, according to a recent survey. Those people bring religion with them, and so the world is also becoming increasingly religiously diverse. You are more likely to be in touch with people in other religions today than you were a hundred years ago.

That's good news, because we want more contact with people in other religions. By the way, the most religiously diverse country in the world is Singapore, where I have lived on occasion; there's no one dominant religion in Singapore. There are Chinese religionists, Islam, Hinduism, and Christianity, all of which are sects of approximately the same size. There's a lot of diversity in Singapore, and the world is moving in that direction, as well.

Surveyors recently asked Singaporeans how they felt about this diversity. Nine out of 10 said they are comfortable living and working with people of other ethnicities and other faiths. That's the future of the planet, actually. As Christians, we should be in a place where we get along just fine with people in other ethnic groups and in other religions.

Another big change is that in 1800, 33% of the world was either Christian or Muslim. Did you know that this number will soon be 66%? This means that, from 1800 until maybe a few decades ago, it went from a third of the world's population to two-thirds. That's a huge change, and that means that the relationship between Christians and Muslims is a very, very important relationship. No matter who you are in global Spirit-filled Christianity, you should be doing something in relationship to Muslims, because these two communities are the largest religious communities in the world.

Then, finally, we want to ask what's happening in mission. Our research has shown that 87% of all Muslims, Hindus, and Buddhists do not personally know a Christian. This is our biggest challenge. As we go forth, we're part of an incarnational faith, of which friendship and hospitality are central values. We believe that Holy Spirit empowerment is going to lead you to engage with people of other faiths.

We've already seen from the research that Spirit-empowered Christianity leads people into taking action in causes of social justice. That's part of who we are. We are people who engage with other people; we're people who help other people; and this is the future of religion, especially as it relates to other large religious communities with whom we're largely out of touch. This is one of our biggest challenges going forward.

As we meet in Jerusalem, let's embrace the fact that Spirit-empowered Christianity will give us the opportunity to change the world. After all, that's why we've all been baptized in the Holy Spirit and empowered by the Holy Spirit —to change the world for God's kingdom.

HOW TO FAIL (OR SUCCEED)

Dr. George Wood

It's my joy today to greet you. I'm George Wood, and along with Dr. Billy Wilson, I'm co-chair of Empowered21. We bring together charismatic and Pentecostal leaders, ministers, and laity from across the globe. The reason we come together is not simply to be at another meeting; it's to energize, mobilize, and equip the Spirit-empowered community to reach this world for Jesus Christ.

In fact, we have an audacious goal: that by 2033—which marks 2000 years since Jesus rose from the dead—every person on planet earth will have had an opportunity to have an authentic encounter with Jesus through the person and power of the Holy Spirit. That is indeed an incredible goal, given the fact that over 2 billion out of the nearly 8 billion people on this planet live outside the reach, walk, and distance of a local church.

So we're talking about an incredible task that lies before us. I've been searching my own heart for how is this going to happen. What is going to enable the Spirit-empowered community to reach this incredible goal? My mind goes back to an incident in the gospels that I want to use as the frame of reference for what lies ahead. Although we may have goals and dreams and aspirations, ultimately, it is God working through us that accomplishes them—that gives us the ability to reach this globe and every person on it with the message of Jesus Christ. The gospel incident I have in mind has to do with one of the 35 enumerated miracles of Jesus.

If you eliminate the duplications of miracle accounts that occur from gospel to gospel, only one of the 35 miracles is found in all four gospels, and that's the feeding of the 5,000—the miraculous feeding of the crowd on that spring day in Galilee, when Jesus had them sitting in groups of fifties and hundreds, and the disciples distributed five loaves and two fish that fed the multitude. I've asked myself the question, "Why, of all the miracles of Jesus, is this the only miracle found in all four of the gospels?" I believe the answer is simple: it is a teaching miracle. It is more than a description of an event that happened; it is a description of how God does his work, how Jesus builds his kingdom, and therefore, it is a miracle about spiritually feeding the world—not just physically feeding a crowd.

In fact, the John 6 account of the feeding notes that the word "great" is used twice of the crowd, and the word small is used twice of the resources: great crowd, small fish, small loaves. I think that gives us a key to understanding how the Lord is going to do his work over the next few years, as we approach (if Jesus tarries) the year 2033. I would simply say that what I'm communicating on this broad level could also be applied on a personal and individual level, to your own life. I have a little bit of a twist on my title, which is simply, The Feeding of the 5,000 Teaches Us How to Fail or How to Succeed.

The first lesson is that the size of the task will always seem great. This is the problem with reaching our culture and our world. The task of world evangelism is an enormous one. How do you reach a secular Europe—a post-Christian Europe? How do you reach the Buddhist world? How do you reach the Islamic world? How do you reach the Hindu world? How do you reach the animus world? How do you reach into cities and villages and tribes where there is not a single Christian congregation? When we look at the size of the task, it can immobilize us. It can cause us to simply sit back and adopt a lethargic or a passive attitude that says, "This simply cannot be done. The task is too big."

I'm sure that's probably how the disciples felt on that spring day, when this huge crowd of people was sitting on a hillside. 5,000 men, plus women and children, were all looking around hungrily, with nothing to feed them except a little boy's lunch of five small loaves and two small fish.

So how do we learn to fail from this story? What causes failure? Looking at the enormity of the task. This is true in your own personal life, as well. When the Lord calls you to do something, if it's bigger than your ability, it's probably a good clue that the Spirit is in it, and wants you to do it. The second lesson is simply this: If the size of the task is enormous, then the resources will always seem inadequate. The resources will always seem small. So how do we fail? Looking at the resources as compared to the size of the task.

This miracle of feeding the 5,000 probably happened one year before Christ's death and resurrection, in the spring. We know that the Passover would have occurred in the spring, as well. So we're one year before Jesus's passion. One year later, 40 days after Jesus ascends into heaven, the disciples are going to face an enormous task, which we call the Great Commission: "Go into all the world, make disciples of all nations, teaching them to do whatever I've commanded you to do." This is an enormous task. Now, it's no longer a crowd of 5,000 men plus women and children. Now, it's the entire world of the first century, which, it's estimated, was about 250 million people.

How are 120 Spirit-empowered people going to reach a global world of 250 million people when they don't have any resources? They don't have any of the modern tools of communication that we think are important today. They are limited by word of mouth and by how fast they can travel (probably 15 to 30 miles a day at the maximum). This task is enormous: it's one Spirit-filled believer for every 2,083,333 people. Think of those odds. That would be like looking at the population of the United States, which is a about 330 million people, and trying to reach them with 120 people in a single generation.

The other way to fail is leave the Lord out of the picture—to forget that the Lord is there to take the little bit we have and multiply it to feed the world. If our task of reaching this world for the Lord Jesus is going to be done by 2033, it is going to take the Spirit's work over and beyond what we can do. It is going to take signs and wonders. It is going to take anointing and a tremendous infusion of the Spirit's power into the life of the church.

Now, quite frankly, had I been one of the 12 that day when Jesus said, "Now take this little boy's lunch and go feed the multitude," I would have been very skeptical that they could be fed. In fact, we know at the end of the miracle that they had 12 baskets leftover. So I'm going to assume that the disciples were the ushers. They were the waiters for the crowd. I imagine them coming to Jesus, who has the little boy's lunch, with their twelve empty baskets. If you take five loaves and break them into 12 pieces, that's about 40% of one loaf for each basket, or disciple.

If you have two small fish, that's one sixth of a fish per disciple. I can almost see the looks of the twelve disciples as they gaze at these meager portions inside their baskets: they see mostly basket. I can imagine Thomas looking at Jesus and saying, "We're supposed to go feed the crowd with this? I mean, look at my basket! There's a sixth of a fish and about 40% of a piece of bread. This is not going to do it. This, this won't even be enough to feed the first guy in the first row."

They probably said, "I'll tell you what, Jesus: if you want to do a miracle here, I have a good idea. Why don't you take this fish and make a pile of fish over here, several feet high, several feet across. Do the same thing with the bread over there. We'll fill up our baskets with fish and bread. We'll serve the first row. We'll come back and refill. We'll serve the second row and we'll continue to do that until we come to the very back. By that time, all the fish and bread will be gone, and everyone will have had enough. Lord, would you please do your miracle that way, that way we can see before we start out?"

I can see Jesus smile at Thomas and say to him, "No, Thomas. That's not how I do my miracles. And that is not how I'm going to build my kingdom. You want to start out with a lot and end up with nothing. I will always start you out with a little and make sure you end up with more than enough."

That's how the Lord builds his church. That's how the Lord builds his work in your life. That's how this task of reaching the world with the gospel is going to get accomplished. If we simply look at what we have now, we'll never get started. We'll be discouraged by how big the task is, and how few of the resources are. But if we trust that the Lord is able to take whatever we put into his hands, then we focus on him, and this task will get done.

ABLAZE—A PROPHETIC CALL TO IGNITE THE CHURCH

Some of you know that I am the son of pioneer missionaries to Northwest China and Tibet. My early years were spent there, before the country closed to missionaries. I remember when I was a boy of eight, our last day in a certain city, where my parents had labored to plant a church. There were probably about 200 believers in that church, along with two other churches in town—probably 500 believers in all. We had to leave practically on a moment's notice and flee. For the next three decades, my parents waited to hear word from the church which they had helped to establish. They neither heard from that church, nor got a word back in. It was simply closed. It was only after my father died that I was able, for the first time, to get back in. I've been back to that town a total of six times now. Do you know what I found? The pastor that had preached the last Sunday I was there, was still there preaching.

Thirty-nine years had gone by since I had seen this man. I remember sitting down with him in the church on a Thursday morning. They had been able to reopen, because the laws now permitted them to have an above-ground church. I said, "Pastor Mung, tell me about what happened to you."

He said, "Well, after your parents left, within a few years, all three of the churches came together as one congregation. I was their pastor, and then I was arrested and sent to prison for nine years." Pastor Mung had a lot of missing teeth— I thought this was probably a result of both malnutrition and prison. Cautiously, I asked, "What did they feed you those years in prison?"

He smiled really big and said, "Well, mostly they fed me spoiled food." I thought, *Wow, if I'd eaten spoiled food for nine years, I don't know if I'd be smiling about that.* He said, "Finally, they let me out of prison. They put me on probation. Sixteen more years went by. We were not allowed to meet as a church. I would go privately to individuals to try to strengthen them. But that was all I could do. Finally, I was called before the authorities and they told me that they had made a mistake in prosecuting me and sentencing me to prison. They gave me my official papers of exoneration."

He said, "I looked across the room at those party officials and said, 'You took away the best 25 years of my life, and all you think you have to do is to apologize?' They were surprised at my response, and made the mistake of saying, 'Well, what do you want us to do for you?' I said, "Number one, I want to preach the gospel again. Number two, I want the church to be reopened and allowed to meet. Number three, I want my granddaughter to have permission to travel across provincial lines and help us, because we're elderly now." He was 72 at the time. "And fourth, all these years you deprived me of income; you should pay me money, or a pension."

They conferred, and gave him what he asked; but in returning the church property to him, they only gave him legal rights—not actual possession. There were squatters on the property. When the pastor went to get them off the property, they beat him up. He told me it took three years to get them off the property. Finally, at the age of 75, he reopened the church, which had been closed for 39 years.

I said to him, "Pastor Mung, how many people did you have?" He said 30, and my heart sank. I thought, *Wow. They used to have 500 believers in this town. Now we're down to 30.* They were mostly older people. I thought to myself, *This church is going to die.*

ABLAZE—A PROPHETIC CALL TO IGNITE THE CHURCH

A 75-year-old pastor, with 30 old people. I knew a little bit about the political atmosphere. They weren't allowed to have meetings for anyone under the age of 18; they weren't allowed to baptize anyone under the age of 18. Everyone over the age of 18, they baptized. They had to turn their name and address and occupation over to the government, in order to be registered as Christians.

He said, "Would you like to see our baptismal roster?" I thought *Probably two or three old people got baptized before they died or something.* His wife went to the little side room, and brought out something I'll never forget. It was a little black cover, with a white material—almost like linen, in between, held together by yarn. I opened it.

The first page was full of writing: five columns—name, age, gender, address, and occupation. There were about 18 to 20 names. I thought, *They've really done great.* I turned the second page: full of names. Third page: full of names. Fourth page: full of names—on and on and on.

I thought, *I'm holding the book of life of my hometown.* Finally, I closed the book and handed it to pastor Mung. I said to him, "How many believers do you have now in this church?" He said, "We have 1,500 adult baptized believers."

I asked in shock, "How did this happen?"

He looked at me like I'd asked a stupid, American question. We like to ask things like, "What seminar did you attend? What book did you read? What successful church did you consult? What are the five steps of revitalizing a church?" All that's well and good, but he looked at me like I had asked one of those American technique questions. He smiled really big and said, "Jesus Christ is the same yesterday, today, and forever, and we pray a lot."

He went on to describe some of the things the Lord had done in that town—miraculous healings. A communist party official's wife had been sent home from the hospital, dying of cancer. They secretly called for pastor Mung to pray for her. He did, and God raised her up and she was healed. Here was a church that, in five years, grew from 30 old people to 1500 adult, baptized believers—a church that couldn't have evangelistic meetings outside of church property. They couldn't pass out literature. They couldn't do street evangelism. They couldn't do coffeehouse evangelism. They couldn't do anything on the Internet. They simply prayed a lot and depended upon the power of the Lord. He took the small resources they put in his hands, and multiplied it. The last time I checked, the Christian community in that town had over 15,000 believers and a Bible school. Pastor Mung has since gone to be with the Lord, but the church continues to thrive and to grow.

To me, it's a marvelous example of the paradigm the Lord wants to show us in these next years. As we head for 2033, if we want God's kingdom to grow—if we want to see this world reached for Jesus Christ—then as Spirit-empowered believers, we must avoid looking at the size of the task. That will only immobilize us. We must avoid looking at the small resources we have. That will only discourage us. Instead, we must look to the One who empowers us to do the work he has called us to do. I pray that this teaching and this story will be an encouragement to your life—an encouragement that what the Lord has called us to do can be done in this generation.

THE EVERYDAY BELIEVER

Andy Byrd

Hi, my name is Andy Byrd, and I'm coming to you from Youth With a Mission Kona. I'm also privileged to be part of the GEA—the Global Evangelistic Alliance—as well as the Send Collaboration.

I'm really excited to share my sense of what God's doing around the world today. I have the privilege of being in lots of different nations, much like many of you that are reading this. I just want to share a few basic thoughts on words that I'm hearing around the world—things that I'm watching take place in front of me right now.

First, I want to share from Matthew 9:35-38. This is a familiar passage to many of us—it gives us a snapshot of Jesus's life on earth. Let's take a look at it together.

"Jesus went throughout all the cities and villages, teaching in their synagogues and proclaiming the gospel of the kingdom and healing every disease and every affliction. When he saw the crowds, he had compassion for them, because they were harassed and helpless, like sheep without a shepherd. Then he said to his disciples, 'The harvest is plentiful, but the laborers are few; therefore pray earnestly to the Lord of the harvest to send out laborers into his harvest.'"

At the beginning of this passage it says that Jesus is walking through towns and villages. We know from background studies that the towns and villages of Jesus's day weren't necessarily easy places to see. You may not have looked at them and said, "This place is fertile soil for a move of God." In fact, we know that 70% of the population was living in poverty, which is an astronomical rate. We also know that there was intense racism in Jesus's day between different ethnic groups that, quite honestly, hated each other.

We also know that oppression was massive. In Jesus's day, the Roman government was an oppressive empire. The Jewish religious leaders were oppressing the followers of Judaism. Women were quite oppressed by men in society; and children were also quite oppressed by adults. You could probably look at any snapshot of Jesus's time and see oppression, racism, and poverty everywhere. This is what Jesus sees.

Then it says that he goes into the synagogues. We know that synagogues were not like "on fire" churches. He wasn't walking into the back of a building and going, "My gosh, the worship in here is hot!" He wasn't walking into an enthusiastic youth group. He didn't come to the preacher preaching repentance and revival. No, Jesus came into the backs of synagogues and encountered condemnation. They were full of heavy-handed teaching; hypocrisy was everywhere. That's the church of Jesus's day.

It goes on from there and says that Jesus proclaimed the good news of the kingdom—that He healed every disease and sickness. Now, that's an amazing statement. The power of Jesus broke out for healing. But you've got to track with Jesus the moment before the healing breaks out, and see what he's seeing and feeling. When Jesus is healing the sick, it means that he's among the sick—and he's not in nice hospitals. They're not getting good nursing care. They don't have a good doctor staff that's overlooking them. No, they're lining the streets of their towns and cities. They're begging for their livelihood. Many of them might be carried there by a family member and left all day long to beg, before being carried home at night. These are the sick ones that Jesus is healing. It's remarkable that he's healing them. It's an overwhelming sight to see if you're walking the streets of Jesus's day.

Then it says that he looks up and sees the crowds, the common people, walking down the streets. And they were harassed and helpless, like a sheep without a shepherd. You can feel and see the overwhelming streets, lined with the sick. Then, as if you were to look up at society around you, Jesus says they're harassed and helpless. In other words, they're full of anxiety. They're full of fear. They may be full of depression. They're struggling under the weight of racism and oppression. There's all kinds of social dynamics going on, to the point where Jesus says they're harassed and they're helpless. Nobody is there to help them. The synagogues aren't helping them. The government is not there to help them. Their spiritual leaders aren't helping them. They're helpless —they're leaderless. This is the scene of Jesus's day. I feel this is so important for us right now, as we look at our nations today.

We can read the headlines, at a fairly universal level, and be overwhelmed by all that's going on: hatred, people living as refugees, rumors of wars or battles going on, immorality, another failure of a Christian. It can be overwhelming. We can read or watch the news, walk our streets, and think, "Is there any hope?" And our response, often, is to retreat to the safety of our home or our small group or our church and say, "You know what? I don't know. It just seems to be getting worse. I sure hope Jesus breaks in." However, that's not what Jesus does.

First of all, he looks at everything he has seen. The first thing that he says is that the harvest is plentiful. Now, I don't know about you, but I don't know if I would have seen what Jesus saw that day and declared the harvest to be plentiful. I don't know if I'd have watched all that was going on and thought to myself, "My gosh, it's just so ripe for a move of God." I think I might've looked at it and gone, "My gosh, is there any hope? What is the hope for this society?"

And yet, Jesus looks at all of that with different lenses. He has different glasses. I think one of the things God is doing in this hour of history is giving the church different lenses with which to look at the brokenness of society, so that we say along with him, "The harvest is ripe."

We can look at impossible situations and declare that the harvest is ripe. We can read the headlines and see them as a longing for hope. We can see that, the more that evil rises up, the more people are looking for an answer. At times, we can live with the mentality that the lost are resistant to Jesus; but I would propose to you that they might be resistant to religion. However, they are longing for a Messiah. They're longing for a hope, and they're looking everywhere for it. Jesus had different eyes. I think today, right now, God is giving us different eyes—to look into brokenness and say, "There is a solution, and his name is Jesus."

Secondly, he goes on to say that harvest is plentiful, but the workers are few. "Ask the Lord of the harvest to send out workers into his harvest field." In chapter 10, Jesus calls his 12 disciples. He gives them authority and sends them out. Now, this is historic. The second thing I see happening all over the world is that, when Jesus does this, he forever changes history.

For thousands of years up to this point, the kingdom has primarily advanced through three types of people. Look at the Old Testament. Every time God needed to speak, to move, to heal, to do something remarkable, he often moved through three people: a king, raised up to lead his people; a prophet, raised up to speak the word of the Lord; and priests, raised up to atone for the people through the sacrificial system. These three types of people were a go-between for God and the people and throughout the Old Testament.

But here in Matthew 9—10, he shifts all of human history. He looks at a harvest field, in which he sees opportunity and brokenness, and he says, "I'm going to do it differently this time. I'm not about to raise up a king. I'm not just looking for a prophet. I don't need someone who carries the title of priest or comes from the family of Levi. I'm doing something far more dangerous. I'm giving my authority to everyday common believers, and I'm going to fill them with an uncommon authority and an uncommon spirit. They will become the answer to the crisis of their day."

This was historic. When we're confronted with the crisis around us, we can say, "I hope my pastor does something about this. I hope an evangelist does something about this. I hope a worship leader could just crush this moment and lead us into the glory." We're looking for these people that we place on pedestals—that have big Instagram followings or big voices or big YouTube channels. In a way we've said, "Our hope is in their abilities," without realizing that Jesus says, "No, I'm not raising up just a worship leader. I'm not just looking for a pastor. I'm not just looking for someone who you see as a leader, an evangelist, or someone extremely articulate. No. I'm raising up something far more dangerous.

I'm raising up dads and moms and 16-year-olds and carpenters and videographers. I'm raising up teachers and politicians and bankers and businesspeople. I am putting my Spirit in them, and I am making the common uncommon through an impartation of my authority, power, and Spirit." This is what Jesus is doing today. He's empowering the entire church to be in the game of the Great Commission—the kingdom spreading across the earth.

This is not the hour for a few names, microphones, stages, and songs or sermons. This is the day of the everyday common believer rising up in the authority and the power of God to be the solution to the crisis of their hour.

The third thing, and the last thing, I would say that I see happening all over the world goes back to the passage in Matthew. Jesus, when confronted with all of the helplessness around him, does several things. First, he has eyes to see. Second, he commissions this new breed of everyday believers. Third, in the midst of all of that, his heart is moved with tremendous compassion and love.

It's easy to get frustrated with the lost for being lost. It's easy to get mad at sinners for sinning. We can get frustrated with the headlines, a generation, or a certain group, instead of moving with compassion and love. How can the lost live like a man they've never met? How can someone trapped in addiction walk in a freedom they've never met? How can sinners stop doing something when they've never met the man who could set them free? Jesus wasn't frustrated with the brokenness of his day. He was moved with compassion. The third thing I see happening all over the world is that God is baptizing his church in compassion.

He's baptizing his church in love—not where we compromise the Word of God, but a compassion for those who have not yet had their lives transformed by the power of the gospel. This love is not love at an arm's distance. It's not love that's "way out there." This love is nearer. The best way I can describe it is it's *adoptive* love.

Adoption is powerful for many reasons. But here's one of the reasons that adoption spans far beyond simply bringing a child into a home. Adoptive love is, in many ways, the highest form of love, because it's love that looks down at a broken situation. Let's look at Jesus moving in adoptive love. He looked at the brokenness of the world—the sickness, the sin, the immorality—and says, "I didn't cause any of this. I didn't make any of this happen. I'm not the Genesis of the sin and brokenness. But I will take responsibility for it."

Jesus takes responsibility for a brokenness he didn't cause. And because of this, we have redemption and the forgiveness of our sins. When adoptive love hits the church, the church is able to look at a city and go, "I didn't cause the brokenness of this city. I'm not the reason that there's poverty. I'm not the reason that there's prostitution. I may not be the reason that this brokenness exists, but I will take responsibility for it—and not just a distant responsibility. I'm willing to bring this brokenness near to my life in order to see transformation through compassion and adoptive love."

This is the heart of every missional movement in human history. Think of Hudson Taylor, who went to China in the days when very few believers were known to be anywhere in that nation; it was dangerous, and many died. Taylor lost many close family members. He could have looked at the brokenness of China and said, "I've never been there. I've never met someone from China. And that is not my responsibility. I didn't cause the brokenness and the lostness of China." However, that's not adoptive love. Adoptive love caused Hudson Taylor to say, "I didn't cause the brokenness of China, but I will take the responsibility for the brokenness of China." And because of it, he brought the nation near to himself. Today, there are more believers in China than any nation on earth, because a man moved in adoptive love.

You can see this again and again throughout history. Some of our favorite heroes of history were those who moved into a radical, mature, gritty love that was adoptive in nature. God is baptizing his church in this kind of compassionate, adoptive love. When we hear about a school shooting, we're not just frustrated; we're not just blaming others. We say, "That school is my responsibility. I'm carrying hope. I carry the gospel. I may not have caused that shooting, but I can take responsibility for it and be willing to embrace the lost." Gone are the days where we can criticize in inactivity. Gone are the days where we can point fingers and go, "I can't believe they did that."

No way. Not anymore. We are called to be moved with compassion. The brokenness of our cities is our responsibility. We've often defined maturity as someone who takes responsibility for their own actions; but I want to say to you that this is the low bar of maturity; the high bar of maturity is someone who's willing to take responsibility for someone else's actions.

These three things in my heart and mind are three of the things I see God saying today across the earth, and across the body of Christ. He's giving us hope-filled lenses to see crisis as an opportunity, and to know that there's a solution. He's giving us the revelation that the solution is not just a few people with big ministries and big names—the solution is the common believer filled with an uncommon power. We're not just moving in robotic ministry. We're not just doing what we think we should do. We are moved with compassion. We are moved with adoptive love. And as we move in that adoptive love, lives are transformed; revival and reformation begin to break out. Dream with me today: What would it look like if these three things marked the entire global church, and the Great Commission was moved into the center of the conversation of Christianity?

A PARADIGM SHIFT

Billy Wilson

Hello, I'm Dr. Billy Wilson, global co-chair for Empowered21, which has become the largest relational network in the history of Spirit-empowered Christianity. Now, when we say Spirit-empowered Christianity, we mean Pentecostals, charismatics, and people all over the world who believe in the power of the Holy Spirit. What God did in the book of Acts, Empowered21 has been designed to continue. Today, I'm going to be sharing about the future of this movement, and how God is shifting things in our generation.

Sociologists tell us, in studying our movement of Spirit-empowered Christianity, that there was a first wave from the Azusa street revival. Traditional Pentecostalism sprang up. It was a wave of the Holy Spirit. Then, there was a second wave, with the charismatic renewal in the 1960s and 1970s. All kinds of churches, including the Catholic church, were affected by the moving of the Holy Spirit during this second wave. Then, there was a third wave in the 80s, 90s, and early 2000s, as independent congregations sprang up all over the world, believing in the power of the Holy Spirit—in healing and miracles and in what God could do today.

I believe that we may be on the precipice of a fourth wave—a new move of the Holy Spirit that will change the world in dramatic ways. This fourth wave hasn't been defined yet, but we see indications of it on the horizon. I asked the student body at Oral Roberts university, "What do you think about this fourth wave? What will be some of the qualities of this new moving of the Holy Spirit?" The number one thing they shared with me was that this new move of God will, first of all, be about unity among believers. Today, I pray that, as you read this teaching, your heart will be fused together with people all around the world who believe that we are in the midst of a shift—a new shift of Holy Spirit power on a new generation.

Empowered21 is about some simple things. It's about world evangelization. Our big vision is that every person on earth would have an opportunity to know Jesus by the year 2033, the 2000-year anniversary of Pentecost, which is recorded in Acts chapter 2. Empowered21 is also about Christian unity—it's about the next generation and the power of the Holy Spirit. If you believe those things, you've tuned in to the right place. Now, I want to do some teaching about this next, fresh shift.

I want to begin by talking about how God brings a shift in our world. Zachariah 2:13 says, "Quiet everyone! Shh! Silence before God. Something's afoot in his holy house. He's on the move." Acts 19 says, "Repent, then, and turn to God, so that your sins may be wiped out, that times of refreshing may come from the Lord." Now, God has always been moving in history. In fact, from the very beginning, when the Bible tells us the world was without form and void, the Holy Spirit was moving on the face of the deep. When God commanded, the Holy Spirit brought about what the Father intended in our world. So God has always been moving; and yet there are times in human history when there is an intensification of the moving of God. I personally believe we're in one of those times of intensification now.

Now, when God intensifies his work in the earth, he shifts things. He moves them from one dynamic to another dynamic—from one phase or stage to another phase or stage. I believe that we are, right now, in an amazing supernatural shift in the world, and I want to talk about that shift. In fact, I want to look at one of the greatest spiritual shifts in biblical history. It's the shift that takes place as we enter the New Testament. When we reach the book of Matthew, God, in many ways, had been silent for almost 400 years, between the book of Malachi and Matthew. During this time, when it appears God was silent according to canonized Scripture, he was at work. He was answering prayer. He was ministering to people; he was healing the sick, he was doing his work in the earth; yet we see, as we enter into the gospels that an intensity starts to take place as God begins to shift things.

I want to look at this shift from the Old Testament to the New Testament—from the days of old to the days of new—from the old covenant to the new covenant—in order to understand the principles at play when God is shifting things. I believe God wants to shift things in our generation, so we need to learn the lessons from this most cataclysmic shift that happened during the time of John the Baptist.

The ministry of Jesus was a paradigm shift. The definition of a paradigm shift is an important change that happens when the usual way of thinking about or doing something is replaced by a new and different way. Now, in the last generation, there have been political paradigm shifts, technological paradigm shifts, and sociological paradigm shifts, as the way of thinking in the world has shifted dramatically. I believe we're in one of these paradigm shifts presently, especially in the Spirit-empowered or Spirit-filled movement.

Let's think about what happened between the book of Malachi and the book of Matthew that brought about such a significant shift, and what will happen in the 21st century as we experience a supernatural shift. First of all, when God is shifting things, there are fresh visitations from heaven. When we start the New Testament, we see that God begins to visit people in a new way. Zachariah is a priest. He's in the holy place with God, and God visits him by the angel Gabriel. Gabriel says to him, "You and Elizabeth are going to have a son. You're to name him John, and he's going to be a messenger from heaven. He's going to usher in the kingdom of God and make a way for the Messiah."

This was startling. It was amazing. Right after that, there is a fresh visitation to a little girl, a young virgin named Mary. The angel tells her, "You're going to bear the Christ child into the world, and you're going to be favored among all women for all of time." These fresh visitations happen when God is about to shift things. God was on the move, and so he was visiting in new ways. Every time in my life that God is getting ready to shift me from one ministry to another ministry —from one direction to another direction—he visits me in fresh ways. Something about these fresh visitations of God wake our heart up and get us ready for the shift God wants to make in our life. So if you need a shift today—if you're stuck in the past, or stuck in where you are—I'm praying that God will give you a fresh visitation.

The second thing that happens when God is shifting things is that we experience a fresh openness to new things, and to what God wants to do. When God visited Zachariah at the temple area and told him that Elizabeth was going to have a baby, it startled Zachariah. He had a hard time believing it; and because he did not believe the messenger initially, the messenger said, "The sign will be that you will not be able to speak until the child is born." Zachariah staggered out from the holy place before the congregation of the people, and he could not speak. So he tried to tell them what's going on. This visitation from God produced new openness in Zachariah. Nine months later, the baby is born. All of this time, Zachariah has been unable to speak; and when they name the child, the entire community thinks he's going to be named Zachariah Jr. But Elizabeth says, "No, I think he's supposed to be called John." So they go to the father, and give him something to write on and say, "What is the baby's name supposed to be" He wrote on the tablet, "His name is John." Now this is significant because, when he declared what God had told him about this child, he got his voice back. Immediately, his mouth was open and he began to speak. He received the new thing. He was open to what God was doing in a new generation, and it gave him his voice.

Let me say to you clearly: we must open up to what God is doing in a new generation if we're going to have a voice with them. In many ways, the church has lost its voice with the new generation because we're stuck in the past. We think God is going to do it like he's always done it. But in this case, God was not doing it like he'd always done it. He was giving an old man and an old woman a baby and saying, "Name him differently. Name him John." And when Zachariah agreed with what God was doing in a new generation, he got his voice back.

I believe we can get our voice back with this generation if we're willing to accept what God is doing in their life in a fresh and open way. This is an amazing time. God is raising up a new generation, and the future of Spirit-empowered Christianity is depending on them. You and I, as spiritual fathers and mothers, must receive what the Holy Spirit is doing in them, even when it's different than what we're used to. John the Baptist dressed in animal skins and ate wild honey and locusts. He was weird; but God was using him. His parents, and the community, were required to receive what God was doing in that new generation.

We've been doing some research recently with the Center for Global Christianity at Gordon Conwell Seminary about the Spirit-empowered movement around the world. This movement has grown exponentially in recent years. In 1945, for instance, there were 16 million people in the world that were Spirit-filled or Spirit-empowered. By 1975, there were 96 million. By the year 2000, the turn of the millennium, there were 530 million Spirit-filled, Spirit-empowered people in the world. Now, there are 650 million people on planet earth that are filled with the power of the Holy Spirit. From 1970 to 2000, there was a dramatic growth in Spirit-empowered Christianity. However, in the last 20 years, there has been a leveling off of that growth, which means, I believe, that our movement is in desperate need of a new shift—a fresh move of the Holy Spirit, and a fresh openness to a new generation. When God wants to shift things—and I believe he does in our generation—he visits us in new ways and he requires new openness on our part.

The third thing that I believe is important for us to realize is that, when there's a new shift going on, God looks for fresh repentance. Peter, in preaching on the day of Pentecost, told the people to repent in order to see the freshness of God from heaven and be refreshed in their spirits. Every great move of God—every major shift in Christianity through time—has been preceded and accompanied by a new depth of repentance. Frank Bartleman, the great historian of the

Azusa Street Revival, said, "The depth of our repentance will determine the depth of our revival." When John the Baptist came as the messenger of this new shift from God, his message was repentance.

Matthew 3:1 says, "In those days, John the Baptist came preaching in the wilderness of Judea saying, 'Repent for the kingdom of heaven is near.'" He said, "The kingdom of God has come near. Repent and believe the good news." Now, this word "repentance" comes from the Greek word *metanoia*, which means a change of mind. It's a deep remorse, followed by significant life change—a shift in direction. If we're going to see a shift in what we see from heaven on the earth in our generation, it's going to require deep repentance on our part. What is it that God may be calling for you to repent from? Bitterness? Anger? Hatred? Attachment to the flesh in some unusual way? I encourage you today to repent. Turn away from it. Change your mind about this, so God can send refreshing from heaven.

The 21st century will be characterized by people who are deeply broken before God. The only people who were able to receive Jesus's ministry were those who had repented and were broken—who understood they needed help.

The fourth thing that happens when God is supernaturally shifting things is that there is a fresh work of the Holy Spirit. There was a fresh visitation, a fresh openness, fresh times of repentance, and a fresh work of the Holy Spirit in the times of John the Baptist and the coming of Jesus into the world. God was doing new things. People could say, "I've never seen God do this before," and that was true. It's always true when God is shifting things.

God works in unusual and miraculous ways in the days when he is shifting things. I believe that, in our generation, the Holy Spirit wants to move in a fresh way to bring about a new shift. So many of us are afraid of the moving of the Holy Spirit, because we just don't know what he wants to do. I want to encourage you to be an explorer. Don't be afraid of what the Holy Spirit wants to do in your life, or in your church congregation in this time. I promise you this: if God shifts things where you are, he's going to do some new stuff—stuff you've never seen before. He promises he will do a new thing in our day, and bring a dramatic supernatural shift.

So when God is moving and things are shifting for heaven's sake, we see fresh visitation. We see a fresh openness to what God wants to do. We see fresh repentance, and we see a fresh moving of the Holy Spirit. And finally, most importantly, we see a fresh revelation of Jesus Christ. John 1:29 says, "The next day John saw Jesus coming toward him and said, 'Look, the Lamb of God who takes away the sin of the world.'" God was shifting things between Malachi and the gospels so people could see Jesus, the Son of the living God. Every moment when God shifts things and moves them in a new direction, it's to help us see Jesus in a fresh and new way, so that we understand him in a new depth. It's so that we come to know him better.

The great revival that happened in Wales was dramatic. In a matter of a few months, over a hundred thousand people were converted in a primitive area of Wales. God poured out his Spirit amazingly at the beginning of the 20th century. When you track this back, where was the epicenter? Where was the spark for the revival? It goes back to a prayer meeting at a church in Wales, where one young lady stood up and said, "I love the Lord Jesus with all my heart." Something about the sincerity, the depth of revelation, her love for Jesus, ignited the fire. Now, there was a lot going on. People were praying and preparing for the revival. Evan Roberts had a vision. God was visiting, God was moving; but really it shifted when somebody had a personal revelation of Jesus.

Today, maybe you need a fresh revelation of Jesus. You're sort of on the outside. You're going through the motions; you do the worship stuff; you sing the songs; you hear the messages; you even read your Bible; but you know, somewhere down inside of you, there is a need for a fresh contact with Jesus that you've never had before.

When that happens, God is going to shift things in your situation and in your life. I really believe that, in our generation, we're going to see dramatic supernatural shifts. In order for that to happen, we need a fresh visitation and a fresh openness, especially to the new generation and what God is doing among them. We need fresh repentance. We're going to see a fresh move of the Holy Spirit. And through it all, we're going to see Jesus in a fresh way. So I pray for you today—that you will experience a fresh shift by the power of the Holy Spirit.

Empowered21 is committed to serve this movement, and to empower a new generation. We're going to be doing exactly that in Jerusalem in 2020. I want to invite all of you to join us May 31—June 3 in Jerusalem. May 31 is the day of Pentecost. This year, we're going to be celebrating the power of the Holy Spirit right at the southern steps of the Temple Mount, probably where Peter preached his message on the day of Pentecost. We're going to be asking God for a fresh outpouring of the Holy Spirit, and a fresh shift toward greater world evangelization in our day.

We'll then move to Pius arena in town, the largest basketball facility in Jerusalem. We are expecting thousands of people, literally from all over the world. We don't want you to miss it. I hope to see you in Jerusalem. I believe that the greatest shift in the power of the Holy Spirit remains before us. Our world is in need. People are hurting and broken, and you and I need fresh anointing to touch them for Jesus Christ. Come to Jerusalem, and join with me as we seek God for this fresh shift.

PRAYING FOR A DOUBLE PORTION

Paul Dhinakaran

My precious friend, it's a joy for me to speak to you about what God is doing around the world, and what God is saying about establishing his kingdom on earth. He has asked us to pray without ceasing. Prayer is the key. Prayer moves mountains. Prayer brings God's will on earth.

This is what the Lord has been showing me for the end times. He showed me Revelation 10:7 and 11, which say:

"But in the days when the seventh angel is about to sound the trumpet, the mystery of God will be accomplished, just as he announced to his servants the prophets."

"And I was told, 'You must again prophesy about many peoples and nations and languages and kings.'"

The one thing that struck me was the realization that the prophecy would take place before the mystery is revealed. The Holy Spirit showed me Anna and Simeon, who had prophesied night and day in the temple. Their prophecy was followed by prayer and fasting continuously—almost for 60 years. Anna was doing this, and the only thing she prophesied was, "God is coming into this world in the form of a little child—as a lamb to be slain for the sins of the whole world in the Holy of Holies in the temple." And surely God honored her prophecy, her prayer, and her fasting, and he came into her own hands as a little child—as well as the hands of Simeon the priest.

For Jesus Christ to come back the second time, there has to be prophecy again. This time, the Lord Jesus Christ is not going to come as a little baby. He's not going to come into the temple to be slain as a lamb. He's going to come back as the King of kings and the Lord of lords. He's coming to judge the world; there's going to be no mercy, no grace. There's going to be judgment; and to usher in his second coming, to usher in the mystery—which even Jesus does not know the date and time of—you and I have to prophesy God's plan for the world and pray it into being.

He says, "You will prophesy now to kings," because Jesus Christ has to be ushered in as the King of kings and Lord of lords. Jesus Christ will establish the right kings in every nation to open the nation for the Lord.

In 1 Kings 19, Elijah prophesied that Jehu would be the King of Israel and Hazael would be the King of Syria. Even today, God wants you and me to prophesy his plan as to who should rule each nation. He will reveal it. And when we pray, it'll come into being. The right kings may not be believers, but they will be people whom God will use to build his kingdom in each country.

He says, "You have to prophesy to nations," because he will come as a solution for the whole world. He says, "You will prophesy to peoples," because, unless the gospel reaches the hearts of millions around the world, people cannot be prepared for the second coming of Jesus Christ.

Secondly, the Lord makes us prophesy to nations. The Lord showed me Joseph, who prophesied God's plan to grow food and to save humanity. He revealed how to grow food for seven years through technology, as well as how to preserve it for 14 years to feed the world. He also prophesied a method for distributing food to all the people, and the system of governance. He saved humanity.

This is prophesying to the nations to frame solutions to the human problem. That's why the Scripture says, "In the last days, I'll pour my Spirit upon all flesh. And your sons or daughters will prophesy and your young men shall see visions." This means that they will find solutions to human problems. The anointing that was upon Joseph will come forth through the Josephs of today to find solutions to human problems. The world will know what a loving God we have, who has a solution through the Holy Spirit for the world's problems.

The verse in Revelation also says "You will prophesy to peoples," because, unless the gospel reaches the hearts of millions around the world, people cannot be prepared for the second coming of Jesus Christ. The prophetic grace will be upon the Word of God, which will be preached to the people. The Word will go to meet the needs of the people. That's where God gives compassion to his servants.

When my father saw the Lord in 1962, face to face, the Lord said, "My son, I was moved with compassion for the people when I was in this world. When I saw them, I was moved with compassion, because they were sheep without a shepherd. When I saw them sick and I healed, I was moved with compassion. When they did not have food and I multiplied the food, I was moved with compassion. When I saw how they cried, having lost their loved one to death and I raised them up… my son, I'm giving you my compassion from today. I'm giving you a new heart. You will cry when you hear the burdens of the people; and when you cry, I will come and see your tears and wipe away the tears of the people for whom you would cry." The same heart of Jesus which cried for Jerusalem cried also for the people.

That is the grace God gives. When that compassion flows through us for the people, the solution comes through the word of God, for their souls to be saved, for their bodies to be healed, for their lives to be established, for the curses to go, for the demons to leave them. This power flows through us. The right Word of God goes with compassion, which transforms them and causes them to accept the Lord as Savior and makes them have miracles.

Finally, Zephaniah 3:9 says, "For at that time I will change the speech of the people to a pure speech, that all of them may call upon the name of the Lord and serve him with one accord."

Today, Christendom is divided; but when the Holy Spirit pours the pure language of God's love, there will be unity. Though we go through tribulations as God's children across the world, God will give us a pure language, which will unite everyone who serves the Lord, so that all may serve him in one accord.

This is the manner in which God is moving. Today, across the nation of India, we see this grace flowing. God enabled us to establish a 24-hour prayer tower just across from the parliament of India—just across the prime minister's office and the president's palace—the seat of power. There, we are able to pray day and night, prophesying his will. That's opening doors: millions are finding hope through the love and sacrifice of Jesus Christ across the nation.

Then the Lord showed me to establish a prayer tower in Israel. It has been established in the tallest building—the city tower, on the 20th floor. People are praying twenty-four hours a day for God to bring the right king in each country. We pray for God's solutions to human problems in every nation, and for God's Word to go with power and accuracy through the prophetic anointing—with compassion—to every nation; for souls to be saved; and for God to unite all God's people in each country—to establish God's kingdom.

This is the move of God through prayer, filled with God's compassion and love for the people. This is what God is doing across the world to establish his kingdom. God wants us to cry as Elisha cried, "My master, Elijah, let me have the double portion of the spirit that is upon you. Let me have it today." We cry, Lord, give me the double portion of the anointing that was upon you, Lord. In John 14:12 you said, "The things that I did, you will do, but greater works shall you do when you believe in me today." We will cry and say, "Lord, transform me into your image. The world needs to see Jesus through me. Not I, but Christ who lives in me."

Let Jerusalem2020 be a place where we cry for the grace to be transformed into the image of Jesus to come upon us, and he will answer. He will pour his Spirit upon all flesh, and all shall establish his kingdom. Once more, he will shake the nations—he will shake the earth—the dry land, the heavens, the seas. The desire of the nations will come, and the Lord will declare peace in that place. Silver and gold shall be provided to build his kingdom on it, to build him a throne on the earth as the King of kings and Lord of lords. This is going to be the object of our prayers during Jerusalem2020. Come, let's receive the King, and the Spirit of the King, in our spirit, to be transformed into his image. God bless you.

A FRIEND OF ISRAEL

Jentezen Franklin

I want to let you know why I love and support Israel. Firstly, the Bible says that Israel is a special people because God chose them. Deuteronomy 7:6-8 says, "For you are a people holy to the Lord your God. The Lord your God has chosen you to be a people for his treasured possession, out of all the peoples who are on the face of the earth. It was not because you were more in number than any other people that the Lord set his love on you and chose you, for you were the fewest of all peoples, but it is because the Lord loves you and is keeping the oath that he swore to your fathers, that the Lord has brought you out with a mighty hand and redeemed you from the house of slavery, from the hand of Pharaoh king of Egypt."

The Lord set his love on Israel, not because they were the mightiest, the greatest, or the strongest. He did it because He chose to love them. God doesn't love us because we're valuable; we're valuable because God loves us. God doesn't love us because of the house we live in, the money we have in our account, the achievements we make, the popularity or fame we accumulate…these things never impress God. God does not love us because we're valuable. He values us. We're valuable because God loves us. Israel is a special people. We are called, as believers, not just to love the land of Israel, but also to love the Jewish people. Israel is a nation God created. It is a nation that is God-decreed, God-loved, God-called, God-elected, and God-protected. Israel has a special purpose.

It's Israel that brought us our Jewish Messiah. The New Testament is from the Jews—the story of Christ, born in a manger; the virgin birth; the death on the cross; the propitiation of our sins put on him; the resurrection from the dead—it all goes back to the Jews. Their contribution was the flesh and blood of that baby; and we know God is the one who provided that blood of redemption that cleanses us from all sin. The Jews are special people.

Secondly, they are under a special, supernatural protection. Jehovah of the armies of heaven guards the nation of Israel. They will never be destroyed. They will never give up Jerusalem. They will never be run out of that country again. They will never give it up. The Bible says in Genesis 12:3, "I will bless those that bless Israel. I will curse those that curse Israel." Which side do you want to be on? You could no more destroy Israel than you can destroy the universe and the God who created it, because he said, "I will defend Israel."

Michael the archangel watches over Israel. Psalm 121 says, "He who keeps Israel will not slumber and he will not sleep." His eye is always on that nation. Now, here's what I want to say to you. A church that decides to bless Israel will release supernatural blessing upon that church. A nation with leaders who will bless Israel will release supernatural blessing upon that nation. A family that decides to bless the nation of Israel in a tangible way will release supernatural blessings upon that family.

Let me give you an example again. What does this look like? In the story of Joseph, when the Pharaoh of Egypt—a Gentile nation—reached down into the prison and brought a Jewish boy named Joseph to the palace, he listened to Joseph interpret his dream. Pharaoh heeded the interpretation, and stored up food so that people would be fed in the middle of the famine. The nation of Egypt began to be blessed as this Pharaoh, a Gentile, evil king, blessed the nation of Israel. The law kicked in, and God made Egypt the most powerful, mighty economic and military force on planet earth. This is a historical fact. And when the rest of the world was starving to death, that nation expanded and became greater and mightier because they had leadership that favored and blessed the nation of Israel.

When I was walking through the streets of Jerusalem on my most recent visit, the Lord spoke something to my heart, and I pulled my phone out. It was so real that I stopped. I felt a strong impression, and I didn't want to forget the wording. That's how God speaks to me. Sometimes, he gives me clear wording. On this occasion, I typed it into my phone. The Lord said, "Find what I bless, and bless it, and I will bless you. Find what I favor, and favor it, and my favor will come back on you. I have blessed this nation. I have favored this nation. And if you lead Free Chapel, and the people who follow that ministry, to favor and bless Israel, tell them to look out—the blessing, the favor of God will come on them in supernatural ways."

Let me show you the difference this makes. So the first Pharaoh favors Israel, and Egypt becomes the mightiest nation with the greatest military in the world. But there came another Pharaoh in Joseph's lifetime who knew not Israel, nor their God, nor Joseph. And he began to oppress Israel, persecute Israel, make their life miserable and enslave them. And God said, "I will curse those that curse you." The same nation that was blessed previously, now are the recipients of ten plagues from God. God's power decimates their powerful economy, and they fall to the bottom.

ABLAZE—A PROPHETIC CALL TO IGNITE THE CHURCH

The second Pharaoh started his rebellion by making a decree: "Kill all the male children of the Jewish race by drowning them in the Nile River." God said, "You don't understand. That's my nation. And when you touch them, you touch me." So they did not kill all of them. One of them escaped. His name was Moses. And let me tell you what happened through Moses. That Pharaoh and his military force were swallowed up. They were killed by the water of the Red Sea. Think of it: the mightiest army in the world ended up with their leader, Pharaoh, fish food in matter of minutes. God says, "When you curse Israel, I curse you. When you bless Israel, I bless you."

It's so important that our children and our children's children understand that America has been blessed because our leadership in this nation—up to this point, for the most part—has stood strong with Israel. The day we don't do it, the blessing and the favor of God will come off of our nation.

There's another amazing story in the Old Testament, and it's found in Genesis 30. It's a story about a businessman. I'm about to give you the greatest key to supernatural blessing on your business. Laban was a businessman, and he hired a young Jewish man by the name of Jacob. Jacob would later get into a wrestling match, and have his name changed to Israel. This businessman, who was a Gentile, begin to bless Israel; and he became so prosperous and so blessed that he was stealing from Jacob. He changed Jacob's wages ten times.

Finally, Jacob resigned. He said, "You've stolen from me ten times, and I'm leaving." Notice how Laban, a Gentile businessman, responds: "Please stay, if I have found favor in your eyes, for I have learned by experience that the Lord has blessed me for your sake." You cannot bless Israel without God blessing you.

Can I show you the most astounding story in the Bible about this? To me, this makes this truth come alive. In Luke 7, there's a centurion who has a sick servant. The Bible says that the centurion heard about Jesus, this Jewish rabbi, and wanted him to come pray for his sick servant that he loved very much. The centurion sent the Jewish elders to ask Jesus, because he knew that, as a Gentile, he couldn't even associate with the rabbi. Luke 7:4-5 tells us the appeal of the Jewish elders on this centurion's behalf: "And when they came to Jesus, they pleaded with him earnestly, saying, 'He is worthy to have you do this for him, for he loves our nation, and he is the one who built us our synagogue.'"

The very next verse says that Jesus went with them; and he ultimately healed the servant. Do you know what got his attention? He's a Gentile who loves our nation, and he's building projects in our nation that will comfort our people. And Jesus said, "Well, let me send a miracle right into his house." Jesus sent the word, and the servant got healed instantly, because this centurion loved the nation of Israel in word and action.

I want you to get excited. This is a miracle of God. It's amazing. God says, "I will bless those that bless you." The Jewish people have given us the Word of God. There's not one Gentile who wrote one word in this book. Every word of this book, from Genesis to Revelation, was written by Jewish hands as they were inspired by God. We have a Jewish Messiah, and a God who loves the nation of Israel.

In Romans 11:17-18, Paul says, "But if some of the branches were broken off, and you, although a wild olive shoot, were grafted in among the others and now share in the nourishing root of the olive tree, do not be arrogant toward the branches. If you are, remember it is not you who support the root, but the root that supports you."

ABLAZE—A PROPHETIC CALL TO IGNITE THE CHURCH

He's saying, "I don't want you to boast against the root. I don't want you to say, 'We're more spiritual, and Israel doesn't matter anymore.'" Paul even says this: "Has God done away with the Jews? Has he cast his people away? Certainly not!" So there is a connection, and Paul explains it like this: we are the engrafted shoots. We were not a part of the vine, but God tied us up and gave us life through the branches of the tree. The tree called Calvary gave us life, and grafted us in. Paul says, "When you see that, don't act like the Jewish people are some insignificant thing." As a matter of fact, he said, don't you dare brag against the roots, because the branch doesn't give the roots life; the roots give the branches life. He's saying, "I want the two to stay connected all the time. I want Jews and Christian ministries to reach out and connect, because I want to show them who my Messiah is." We know who he is, we know in whom we believe and we want to see that happen.

The way to make that happen is to show the love of God in tangible ways. That's what I felt the Lord said to me. He said, "I'll prosper anybody who gets involved in this; they'll be astonished."

Joseph and Jesus are beautiful. Joseph in the Old Testament is a picture and a foreshadowing of Jesus. He was his father's favorite son; Joseph was wrapped in his father's favor; he wasn't received by his own. He was stripped and left for dead. But Joseph was raised from the pit, went to the palace, and sat at the right hand of the king of Egypt. Jesus was His Father's Son; He was wrapped in the Father's favor, rejected by His own people, stripped, beaten, and left for dead. He was raised from the pit, and He went to sit at the right hand of God the Father. He was given a name that is above every name, that at the name of Jesus, every knee should bow and every tongue should confess that he is Lord. He holds the keys of death, hell, and the grave. The similarities are clear.

But the part that hasn't happened yet is foreshadowed in the story of Joseph, when his brothers came into the land because they were starving to death. They tried to get food, and Joseph disguised himself. The third time they came into the land, Joseph revealed his true identity to them. Well, the nation of Israel has come into the Promised Land three times. The first time was when Joshua led them in; the second time was after the Babylonian captivity, when Ezra and Nehemiah came back and rebuilt and took the land. The final time was May 15, 1948.

The third visit is when Joseph revealed who he really was to his own brothers; and before he did, made all the Gentiles or the Egyptians leave the room, as a picture of the rapture. That's a picture of the catching away of 1 Thessalonians 4. The church is going to be taken out, and then come seven years of tribulation. But when the church is gone, at the end of the tribulation, when it looks like Israel is going to be wiped out, Jesus is going to appear.

How did Joseph's brothers recognize him? Genesis says that when they saw the scars, they recognized that it was Joseph. That's the part of the prophecy that hasn't happened yet. But there's coming a day, according to Zechariah 12:10, in which "I will pour out on the house of David and the inhabitants of Jerusalem a spirit of grace and pleas for mercy, so that, when they look on me, on him whom they have pierced, they shall mourn for him, as one mourns for an only child, and weep bitterly over him, as one weeps over a firstborn."

There's coming a day when they're going to look at those scars on Jesus's body; and that's the thing that's going to convince them that He is the Messiah—that He is the one who lived, died, rose, and took away our sin. This is what we believe. When Jesus comes back, he's not coming to Paris, France. He's not coming to Washington, D.C. He's going to go ride to a city called Jerusalem. He's going to set up his kingdom, and we're going to rule and reign with him. The Jews are gone, I believe; and we're going to rule and reign with our Messiah. Then, we'll go into the millennial reign. For a thousand years, it'll be so much better than life today. We can't imagine: no more pain, no more sickness. It's just going to be heaven on earth. It's going to be wonderful; and I'm glad I'm not on the losing side. The devil is going down, down, down, and the kingdom of Jesus is coming up.

What I'm preaching to you today is the key to blessing and favor on you, your family, your business, your church, and your nation. If ever a generation needed to hear why we love and support Israel, it's this generation. We're one generation away from electing people who would completely turn their back on Israel—who forget God's promise of blessing. The day America does that, you can know that's the day the favor and the blessing of God will leave. Just as Egypt was washed up in one day, America will follow suit. It's critical that we pray for the peace of Jerusalem, and we say to our Jewish friends, "You're not in the trenches, the tunnels, and the war zone alone; but you have a friend called America, and God has blessed us to be a blessing to you."

THE KEY TO SUCCESSFUL EVANGELISM

Michael Koulianos

My name is Michael Koulianos from Jesus' Image in Orlando, Florida. It's such an honor to be part of what the Lord is doing throughout the world with Empowered21. I'm privileged to talk to you about what I believe the Holy Spirit is saying and doing today in the body of Christ and in the world, as well as what I believe he has planned for 2020.

You know, as of late, we've discovered the beauty of simply loving Jesus. And I believe this is what the Lord is saying. It seems to me that the Lord is genuinely raising up a Jesus movement in the nations and in the earth. He's calling us to radical devotion—devotion that costs us everything. But at the same time, he's bringing a simplicity to this pursuit; and it's liberating—beautiful. The presence of the Holy Spirit is endorsing and charging our gatherings with his anointing. I believe that this Jesus movement is literally of the Lord himself. He is awakening the church to look at him, to love him, to behold him, and to follow him in radical, wholehearted devotion and love.

The Scripture says in Matthew 22:34-40, But when the Pharisees heard that he had silenced the Sadducees, they gathered together. And one of them, a lawyer, asked him a question to test him. "Teacher, which is the great commandment in the Law?" And he said to him, "You shall love the Lord your God with all your heart and with all your soul and with all your mind. This is the great and first commandment. And a second is like it: You shall love your neighbor as yourself. On these two commandments depend all the Law and the Prophets."

So here, a lawyer comes up to up to the Lord and says, "Hey Jesus, what is the most important truth that the law contains? What is the apex of the highest mountain? What is this all about?" It's interesting to me that the Lord does not hesitate to answer the question. I love it. The question is asked, and Jesus responds quickly. And this is his response: "You shall love the Lord your God with all your heart, with all your soul, and with all your mind." Another gospel adds "strength" to this list.

So when you combine heart, soul, mind, and strength, we are talking about the entirety of who we are—the entirety of our being. So here the Lord says, "Loving me with all you are is the first and greatest command." What do I believe the Lord is saying in 2020? I believe he's saying what he's always been saying: "Love me with all you are." That is what he wants. Now, as somebody who values the office of the evangelist—as somebody who hosts massive events—I have a deep value for preaching the gospel and for the great harvest that I believe we've stepped into. I train our people to be on outreach 24/7. So I have a deep value for the Great Commission. It is a mighty Commission. It is a privilege. It is actually a co-laboring with the Lord.

But it's important we understand that it is the Great Commandment that fuels the Great Commission. We don't preach the gospel, heal the sick, cast out demons, raise the dead, cleanse the leper, disciple the nations, and baptize them in the name of the Father, Son and Holy Spirit because *we have to*. No. We do that because we're in love. That's why Paul said, "Woe is me if I don't preach the gospel." What was he talking about? He knew that the Jesus who saved him is worthy of his entire life being surrendered to him.

So simplicity, I believe, is returning to the church in a way we've never seen. The deeper we go with the Lord, the simpler he makes it. Jesus is the gospel. Jesus is the point of the Scriptures. Jesus is the author of the Scriptures. Jesus is the centerpiece of heaven. The life of Jesus is the Good News. The word "gospel" means "good news," and I like to say, "Take Jesus out of the gospel, and the news is no longer good." The gospel was his idea. The gospel is the power of God. So it's his power unto salvation.

What we're watching the Holy Spirit do through all of the incredible ministries that are part of Empowered21 is we're watching the Holy Spirit endorse and bless this Jesus movement. It is bigger than us. It is not about us. It is about him.

As we intentionally exalt the Lord—as we lift Jesus as high as we possibly can—we are watching the Holy Spirit come down upon his people. A harvest is taking place like we've never seen. This is the greatest time to be alive. This is the greatest moment in church history. Stadiums are filling—multiple stadiums on the same day. That tells me something. It seems like we've entered this season where the Lord of the harvest is rising up within us. As someone who deeply values evangelism, I have found—and I'm still discovering—that the key to successful evangelism is Jesus, the great Evangelist, emerging in our hearts. He is arising within his body now, and a massive harvest is in front of us. Stadiums are too small to contain it!

ABLAZE—A PROPHETIC CALL TO IGNITE THE CHURCH

As I said, I believe cities and nations are about to feel the loving tremor of Jesus—the Savior arising—the nations being swept in. This is the greatest time to be alive. It is also the greatest time to fall in love with the Lord. Nobody is as beautiful as Jesus. Nobody is as kind. No one is as loving. No one is as generous. No one is as merciful. Nobody's as powerful. The Scripture says that he is the hope of the nations. His beauty is indescribable. He's a faithful friend, and I want to invite you to commit your heart personally to the Lord himself.

Yes, ministry is important; but at the end of the day, it's his ministry. Yes, events are important; but these events are under him. He gives us the power and fuels our hearts with the faith so that they take place. As the body of Christ, I'm praying that we will turn the affection of our hearts back to the beautiful face of the Lord himself.

Simplicity is a beautiful truth, and I believe it's something that the Lord is giving us. John Wesley said it like this: "Simplicity is the loving devotion to Jesus Christ and Jesus alone." That's it right there. As this happens in us, it begins happening in the body worldwide. This is the Jesus movement. This is what we've been waiting on. And now it's here. I mean, we've been praying for decades, and now we are here; and I feel the Holy Spirit encouraging us, now that we're here, to look at Jesus even more intently.

Let's look at Jesus with a simpler devotion and let's make the Word of God our delight. Let's be intentional about the way we build our families and marriages. Is the presence of God the centerpiece in our home? Am I praying for my children daily? Twice a day, I lay hands on my children, and begin to declare blessings and the Scriptures over them. I've done that since the day they were born. My oldest is 14 years old now. So this is something I'm praying that the church worldwide would commit to—the presence of the Lord in our homes. Are we spending time with the Lord daily? Is our devotion a daily secret place with him? Is it consistent? Are we staying with the Lord until he satisfies our hearts—until a fire erupts within us—until this burning flame begins to overtake us?

This changes our homes. It changes our marriages. It changes our relationships with our children. It changes everything. If we can do this in our homes, the Lord can entrust us with just about anything. At that point, we're authentic and real. Jesus said, "Man does not live by bread alone, but by every word that proceeds from the mouth of God." So are we looking at this precious Word of God as our actual bread? Are we more dependent on the Scriptures than we are on natural food? That's how the Lord wants us to approach his precious Word.

If you're a pastor, I want to challenge you: preach the clearest gospel of Jesus Christ. Let 2020 truly be the year where the Jesus people emerge, and we see this mighty harvest. Preach Jesus this entire year from the Scriptures. Preach the gospel every single Sunday. Give sinners a chance to find redemption in the Lord. If you're a worship leader, I want to invite you to minister to the Lord. Yes, the people are important. The Lord loves the people. But we discovered that people are most loved when Jesus is loved most. And so, as we give the Lord our attention, his presence begins to do what we could never do as we worship Jesus. So sing to the Lord. Ask him for songs that come straight from heaven. Don't stop worshiping until you know the Lord is pleased, and until you know the Lord is in the room.

I'm believing that millions will be born again within the local church this year. As pastors commit to preach the gospel, I want to invite those who are not in full-time ministry to pray for your leaders. Pray that the anointing of the Lord would fall on them. Pray for their families, their strength, and pray that they would be bold proclaimers of the gospel.

So what is Jesus saying? What is the Holy Spirit saying to the church in 2020? This is what I believe he's saying: "Love Jesus Christ." Throughout the Scriptures, we find that this is the greatest achievement in the universe—to love the Lord. If we love the Lord, he will do great and mighty exploits through us, gladly. Look at Jesus. Look at his fullness. Look at his completion. Look at who he is.

What do I believe the Lord is going to do in 2020? A few things. Number one, I believe that the church is going to be electrified with a new revelation of, value for, and love for Jesus Christ. Secondly, I believe that multiplied millions—tens of millions—are going to be swept into the kingdom in 2020. The harvest is ripe. This is the time to get in the game. This is the time to avail yourself. This is the time to surrender and say, "Lord, use my life." We need to believe, as lovers of Jesus, that millions upon millions will be born again this year and fall in love with the Lord Jesus.

Heavenly Father, I pray in Jesus's name that you would touch those reading right now—that you would begin to move on the hearts of the church, and people worldwide, to look at the Lord, to behold the Lamb. I pray, Lord Jesus, for a fresh revelation of your beauty, of your all-sufficiency; and I pray in Jesus's' name that you would thrust forth laborers into the harvest field so that more and more people would fall in love with you, and so that you would know the love of your bride. I thank you Lord. I ask for a blessing to fall upon the people, and I pray your presence on them and in them—in their homes and on their lives. In Jesus's name, amen.

MEN LIKE TREES WALKING

Nathan Morris

This is what the Word of God says in Mark 8:22-26:

"And they came to Bethsaida. And some people brought to him a blind man and begged him to touch him. And he took the blind man by the hand and led him out of the village, and when he had spit on his eyes and laid his hands on him, he asked him, 'Do you see anything?' And he looked up and said, 'I see people, but they look like trees, walking.' Then Jesus laid his hands on his eyes again; and he opened his eyes, his sight was restored, and he saw everything clearly. And he sent him to his home, saying, 'Do not even enter the village.'"

I want to look at verse 23 again: "He took the blind man by the hand and led him out of the village." When God called me, I had an encounter with the fire of the Holy Spirit. I was in a room all by myself—not in a church or listening to a preacher. The Holy Spirit visited me in such an incredible way. I laid on the floor for three hours, under the power of God. You can't tell me that the fire of God isn't real. People try and tell me, "Well, I don't believe in all of that." I don't really care, because you'll never take my testimony. You don't need to tell me that the power of God is real. I know it's real.

ABLAZE—A PROPHETIC CALL TO IGNITE THE CHURCH

I ran from God—did drugs and alcohol. I'd be in the clubs and the bars. I wasn't always just a nice pastor's kid. I was a young man with rebellion in his heart that ran hard from God. But when I encountered Jesus—when I encountered the presence of God on that floor—when I got up, I was never the same. He changed me from the inside out. There was a fire that started to burn in my heart. I didn't use to have a desire for ministry. If you'd have told me as a young man that I would be a preacher, I would have laughed right in your face. But God began to open my heart and I began to see as I bowed to worship the Lord, multitudes of people.

Many of you may have seen the videos of Shake the Nation's gospel campaigns, with thousands of people; but before I saw it on a screen, I saw it in my mind. God opened my eyes to something greater than myself before I ever saw blind eyes opened. When I was in the presence of the Holy Spirit, he would show me people throwing the crutches in the air. It wasn't just my mind; this was God birthing something in my spirit.

Recently, I was in a meeting in Arizona, sitting in the front row. I was just about to preach, and the Spirit of God came on me in that service like a fire. I felt the power surging through me, and the Lord gave me the Scripture from Zechariah 10:1, which says, "Ask for rain in the time of the latter rain. Ask for rain in the time of rain." As I sat there, I said, "Lord, what does that mean?" When you read Scripture, you realize that the latter rain is the end-time outpouring of the Holy Ghost. I want to preach to somebody right now that we're living in those days. This is the hour of the outpouring. I don't know what you're waiting for. The Spirit of God is being outpoured right now. It's here. It's raining. God is saving; He's healing; He's setting the captive free, right now. I don't listen to people that preach what God's going to do in 30 or 40 years. I'm tired of that. I want to know what God's doing right here, right now, in this generation. I'm not waiting for a coming revival; revival's here right now. It's here. It's waiting.

I said, "Lord, what do you mean, 'Ask for rain?' How can you ask for rain when it's already raining?" God spoke this to me: "You must position yourself."

Suddenly I realized that, even though I'm seeing what we're seeing—and I praise God for that—there's something greater God wants this generation to step into. It isn't just about more lights and more smoke machines and better buildings. It's about the presence of the Holy Ghost lighting a fire in this generation. It's raining! God wants to open your eyes to something greater. There's something deeper.

What do you see? What are you seeing in your spirit? What are you seeing in your life? You see, the devil will fight you day and night to try to stop you from seeing God's purpose in your life. You're not here by accident. The Bible says that the Lamb was slain from the foundation of the world. Now, in your carnal mind, you may say, "Well, how does that happen? How could the Lamb be slain before God said, 'Let there be light'?" Because He decreed it from his mouth. He spoke it before he made the heavens and the earth. He'd already decreed that Jesus would die on a cross, that he would shed his blood, that he would rise from the dead.

Why is that important? Because when God decrees something, he decrees it from eternity into time. That's why Galatians 4:4 says, "But when the fullness of time had come, God sent forth his Son." The Word was made manifest from eternity into time. The Bible says that God chose you in him from the foundation of the world—that he'd already decreed your name; and with it, he gave you an assignment. He sent a word over your life; and when the fullness of time had come, you were born to fulfill what God had already decreed from eternity. That's why you're here—that you can see what God has already decreed over your life!

That's what the devil fights me on day and night. He doesn't want me to see what God has birthed on the inside of me. That's what God is doing in your life: birthing something bigger than you. He's already decreed over your life what you will see and what you will fulfill. The moment the Holy Spirit opens your eyes, that's when you're dangerous to the devil.

I don't want to live in the status quo. I don't want to live with somebody else defining my reality. I want to walk with the Holy Ghost, who tells me there's something bigger; there's something greater that no devil in hell can stop. It's something that God birthed in you. He's spoken over you, and there's nothing that can stop it coming to pass.

In Mark 8, they bring a blind man to Jesus. Watch this. Jesus doesn't speak to him. The blind man doesn't even tell him what's wrong with him. Jesus simply takes him by the hand and leads him out of Bethsaida. Jesus then begins a process by which this man would regain his vision. I'm speaking to some people who have lost your focus—your vision. The Holy Ghost is about to open your eyes to something greater than you've ever seen before: a greater harvest, a greater anointing, a greater impact, a greater stature.

Jesus leads him out of Bethsaida. Does this mean that Jesus couldn't just do a miracle in Bethsaida? Of course he could have. He could have *looked* at the man and the man would have seen; but something powerful happened. He takes the blind man, leads him by the hand, outside of Bethsaida. You see, sometimes, when God is about to take you to a new level, you don't ask questions. You just have to follow. Sometimes, even though you can't see a way out, you've just got to follow. If you follow him, he'll lead you to a place where you have an encounter you've never had before. I can take you to places all over the world where I've encountered a new level of the Holy Ghost—a fresh anointing in my life; but there were seasons in which I had to just follow. I couldn't see a way out. I didn't know how I was going to get the money. I didn't know how I was going to get the breakthrough. But I just had to follow. Because Jesus was leading me.

You see, Jesus leads the blind man out of Bethsaida. The Bible says that they brought a blind man to Jesus. There are some people God uses in your life to lead you to him; but there are some people you can't go with anymore if you're going to have a fresh encounter. It's not that they're wrong. It simply means God is trying to bring you to a new place. See, there were some people with me for one season of my life; but then God said, "No, you've got to leave them. You've got to follow me, and you can't rely upon them."

You see, the problem with the blind man was this: he relied on those individuals to define his vision. He couldn't see. They had to see for him. However, there comes a time that you can't rely on somebody else's vision. You've got to see it for yourself. You got to see the harvest. You've got to see the one that said, "I am the miracle-working God." You have to see it. You've got to get the anointing. You've got to start to follow him. The Bible says that we walk by faith and not by sight. Jesus leads the blind man out of Bethsaida, because he is about to have an encounter. He's about to see Jesus like he's never seen him before.

What was it about Bethsaida? You've got to know the word of God for what I'm talking about. You see, Jesus spoke to Bethsaida and he said, "Woe to you Bethsaida, for if the mighty works which were done in you would have been done in Tyre and Sidon, they would have repented long ago, sitting in sackcloth and ashes. But it will be more tolerable for Tyre and Sidon on at the judgment than for you." What was wrong with Bethsaida? They were locked in unbelief.

They saw the power of God; they saw the miracles of Jesus, but their hearts were hardened. Is your environment stopping your miracle? I've learned that there are a lot of people trying to have a God encounter in the wrong environment. In the gospel crusades around the world, the greatest miracles happen when the environment is changed by the power of the Holy Ghost. I've learned that I can try and do it in my own strength; but when he changes the environment, suddenly miracles begin to break forth. You've got to come out of the environment you're in right now. Who are you listening to?

I have decided that I'm not going live with the dream killers. I'm not going to be in that environment. I make sure that who I'm connected to has my DNA, because there's something in you that God has put in me; and when we connect, something powerful begins to happen. You see, sometimes God says, "I've got to lead you out of that environment. I've got to lead you out of that mindset. I've got to lead you out of that thing that is stopping you from seeing me the way I need you to see me."

I remember preachers when I was young—they would tell me, "You know, God does miracles in Africa," as if we had to go on mission to see a miracle. It drove me crazy, because there was something inside of me like a cry, that said, "That is not true. The God of Africa is the God of the nations of the world. What he does for one, he'll do for all. He's a miracle-working God."

I remember in Mobile, Alabama when Delia Knox got out of that wheelchair after being paralyzed for 23 years. CNN and ABC and all the reporters flooded into the revival because a woman got out of a wheelchair; but I had to learn never to allow the environment to shape my faith. It doesn't matter what culture says. It doesn't matter what those voices say. You've got to get into the presence of God, where you know that he defines your atmosphere. When you understand that the Holy Ghost defines your atmosphere, then you're ready to change your environment.

Maybe there are some who have relationships with people from whom you've spent your life trying to get affirmation. It will never happen, because that's not a relationship that God has ordained. And you wonder why your atmosphere now makes you feel like you're not worth it. You don't feel like you're ever gonna make it. The devil is a liar.

Jesus, Jesus, Jesus. It changes your environment. See, when I walk into those stadiums, not everyone's happy to see me. There are some that want me to get out of it. I don't let that environment shape me, because I'm not of this world. I belong to a kingdom in which God says that wherever the souls of my feet tread, I shall possess. That is the power of God in us. I want you to see it.

Jesus said that we've got to deny ourselves in order to follow him. I'm just going to put it like this: you can't deny what your life lives in agreement with. Sometimes we come into agreement with stinking thinking that gives the devil access to our minds and hearts. It's time to move out of that Bethsaida and step into a new environment that lets the power of God begin to release you from the yesterdays that are holding you back.

Jesus spits on the man and he says, "What do you see?" Did you know that spit is one of the greatest DNA profiles?

Does your vision have his DNA?

Does your calling have DNA of the kingdom? Will it count for eternity, or is it all about you and your promotion? You see, God is about to move this generation out of all the self-promotion, into a realm where the Spirit of God says, "This counts for eternity. This is about souls; this is about changing our culture; this is about raising up a standard against the devil."

He said to the blind man, "What do you see here?"

He said, "I see men like trees walking."

I've gone to so many conferences. Some conferences want you to come and give the eight steps, or the four ways, of how to heal the sick. I don't have the eight ways, or the four ways. I only know one way. I don't have four points for a breakthrough. I've heard preachers preach that Jesus had to pray twice in this story because he only got a partial breakthrough.

Really? Jesus could have looked at the man and caused the man's eyeballs to come out, spin three times, change color three times, and go back in his head without opening his mouth.

I said, "Lord, if I'm going to preach this to my generation, show me."

The Spirit of God said, "Stop looking at his blindness and look at the trees."

I said, "Look at the trees?"

I started to study what trees mean in the Word. You see, when the Bible speaks of trees and men, it speaks of being planted—being established and rooted. Jesus was showing the man something greater than his natural vision. He was showing him what he was about to become. God is trying to show you that you're about to be established. You're about to be planted. You're about to be released into your destiny.

You say, "Well, where's the Bible verse for that?" Psalm 1 says, "Blessed is the man that walketh not in the counsel of the ungodly." In other words, blessed is the man that doesn't walk in Bethsaida. Instead, blessed are the men who come out of Bethsaida. The psalm goes on, "...nor stand in the way of sinners, nor sitteth in the seat of the scornful, but his delight is in the law of the Lord, and in his law does he meditate day and night. And he shall be like a tree planted by the rivers of water that bring forth fruit in his season. His leaf shall not wither and whatever he does, he shall prosper."

I see men like trees walking. I see people right now in front of me that God is establishing—not to be taken out, but to stand in our generation and be so rooted that their environment can change their destinies. Be so planted that not even the devil can stop what God is birthing in you. I see men like trees walking, going into all the world and preaching this gospel. Does your vision have his DNA? What do you see?

That's why the devil comes against you. That's why he tries to give you hell. That's why he tries to get to your mind so that you can't visualize what God is speaking to you. The enemy knows that if he can shape this environment so that you get carnal, it will destroy you. But there are those that are hearing the Word. God is breaking that over your life; he's repositioning you into a place of his presence.

Some of you, this next week, are going to go to bed and feel the glory of God coming in your room. Why? Because he's changing your environment. Some of you are going to see more miracles in your heart that God says are about to come to pass in your life. Why? Because you see men like trees walking.

It's time to come out of your Bethsaida. I don't know what voices have power over you; but deny them right now, because God's about to change your environment. He said to the blind man, "Go home, but don't go back to Bethsaida." That means the blind man never lived in Bethsaida. He'd gone there in his blindness, and Jesus came in to bring him out. Jesus came into your life to bring you out!

WHAT DO I SEE IN 2020?

Goodwill Shana

As we begin to prepare for Jerusalem2020, we need to hear what the Spirit of the Lord is saying—much like Elijah. When Elijah began to pray for rain, the Lord spoke to him and showed him something in the horizon: a cloud the size of a man's hand. Elijah went to Ahab and said, "Hurry up, so that the rain does not stop." There are a couple of things the Spirit of the Lord wants us to be aware of, that will help us to hurry and participate in the rain clouds of heaven.

What do I see in 2020? I see a church strengthening an empowered global unity: the church being the church, and doing what only the church can do—releasing anointed, powerful ministry. What do I see in 2020? I see a depth of the work of the Spirit of God in reviving old movements and old places, and the glory of God coming back into the church with a new freshness and outpouring.

What do I see in 2020? I see a revival and a fresh manifestation of the gifts of the Spirit in the pews—in the people—in the congregation—like we've never seen. This is not just a few powerful men standing under the anointing of Almighty God, but the power of God moving into the highways of the byways of our communities. What do I see in 2020? I see a simplicity of ministry that powerfully impacts others. I see the Spirit of the

ABLAZE—A PROPHETIC CALL TO IGNITE THE CHURCH

Lord moving in simple but powerful ways. I see a movement of young people experiencing and sharing the power of the Holy Spirit in ways that jump boundaries, lines, and distinctions, doing what no other generation has done before.

What do I see in 2020? I see revival and a great anointing on the ministry of the evangelist, and the ministry of the teacher. I see God bringing these two roles together in a powerful way, especially amongst young people. We will see younger evangelists and teachers of the Word of God being moved mightily, being used mightily in ways that we haven't seen yet. What do I see in 2020? I see—particularly in Africa—the true, Jesus-centered church rising above the confusion of the pseudo-spiritual and the false prophetic, and reasserting itself in a way based on biblical ministry, teaching, and empowerment. I see the church raising a new standard of biblical church leadership, ministry, and accountability.

What do I see in Africa? I see a strong continental prayer unit movement of apostles and fathers—reputable men and women—coming together under the hand of Almighty God to release unity and joy, and to open heaven in the 12 pillars of society. What do I see for Africa? I see a Spirit-filled move of presidents and governments that will reestablish integrity and morality—that will bring a turnaround in development across the continent. I see a time and season when Africa will enter a window of golden opportunity and revival, through the hand of God on governments and presidents. I see a powerful 2020; a God-anointed 2020. May God help us to be carriers of that anointing—to bring it forth—even as we take time to pray and fast at Jerusalem2020.

God bless you.

A COMMISSION FOR EVERY BELIEVER

Chadwick Mohan

I want to begin by talking about the great commission of Jesus Christ. Jesus called his eleven and he said, "Go into all the world and make disciples of all nations, baptizing them in the name of the Father, the Son, and the Holy Spirit, and teaching them to observe all things that which I have commanded you. And surely I'm with you always, to the very end of this age" (Matthew 28:19-20).

Sometimes we think that this commission is just for the 11; but if it had been a command only for the 11, then only 11 people should have waited for the Holy Spirit. Acts chapters 1 and 2 make it clear that 120 people are waiting for the Holy Spirit. The spirit of God came upon the people who were waiting in the upper room, and filled these 120, who went on to shake the Roman world upside down. This commission is just not for the 11; it was for the 120. And it's not just for the 120.

Peter rises up in Acts chapter 2 and begins to preach. He says, "This Holy Spirit who has been poured upon us is not just for us. It is for your children and for your children's children, and to those who are far off." I believe that "those who are far off" are you seated here—it's us that Peter spoke about; and he said, "The spirit of God is upon everybody."

ABLAZE—A PROPHETIC CALL TO IGNITE THE CHURCH

I want you to know that the Spirit of God is not just falling upon some "special" people. He is falling upon everybody. The church of Jesus Christ has been anointed by the power of the Holy Spirit. If you believe, say, "Jesus, thank you for the Spirit, and thank you for this coming." All of us have been called; but sadly, from the third century onward, we deviated—we grew farther and farther from this truth. In the 21st century, Christianity has become a religion.

Jesus was not about a religion. Jesus was about a relationship with the Father in heaven. Everyone has been given an opportunity to choose the Father—the original father. There is another father, who's called the father of all lies—Satan. Everyone has a choice to make as they grow up. This is about a relationship, but we made it a religion. From the third century to the fifteenth century, we called it Roman capitalism; but the next 500 years, we converted it to Protestantism, or Evangelicalism.

The problem with this liberal religion is that we follow a false teaching. What false teaching? The teaching is that, if you come to Christ, you will get a ticket to heaven. The New Testament does not talk about a "ticket" to heaven. The New Testament talks about following Jesus Christ on a path. And that is why the early Christians in the first century were called the People of the Way—because Jesus is the Way, the Truth, and the Life. People are called to His way, and He says, "Come, follow me." He said, "Don't hesitate. I'm not giving you a ticket to heaven, but I want you to follow me on the path." He promises that, "Where I am, you will also be."

The greatest challenge of the 21st century religion called Christianity is that we think that, somehow, we can get a ticket to heaven and land up somewhere where there's gold. That's not what the Scriptures are talking about. Gold is still of this earth. God is calling us to be with him forever. And his dwelling place is in heaven. This is not about a religion. This is about a relationship. That's why the book of Revelation talks about the people following Jesus as following the shepherd. These people were pure, and they followed the Lamb wherever He went. This is what God is calling us to—He's calling us to be His disciples, and to walk with Him. As we walk with Him, He says, "This is the commission to you, disciples: go into all the world, make disciples of all nations, baptizing them in the name of the Father, the Son and the Holy Spirit, and teaching them to observe all the things that which I have commanded you."

How can I be involved in this mission that Jesus commissioned? This is discipleship. This is commission. This is command. This is not something I should think somebody else will do. No, all of us who are disciples have this commission. It's not just for a few.

The first thing I need to embrace is the priesthood of all believers. In religion, there's a set of people who are priests. Jesus is calling all believers. You are special. Sometimes we think there are people who are specially anointed. We don't have special doors in the kingdom of God. The Spirit of God falls on everybody. We are all anointed by the same special Spirit; we are called to be priests—that's what 1 Peter 2:9 says: "You are a chosen people, a royal priesthood, a holy nation, God's special possession, that you may declare the praises of him who called you out of darkness into the light of Jesus." We are a royal priesthood, and yet, so many of us are stuck in religion and the old covenant.

That's why Hebrews 7:11 says, "Now if perfection had been attainable through the Levitical priesthood (for under it the people received the law), what further need would there have been for another priest to arise after the order of Melchizedek, rather than one named after the order of Aaron?" There was still a need for another priest to come—one in the order of Melchizedek, not Aaron. Jesus brought something better than religion: He brought us the opportunity to come before God as a royal priesthood.

Now that I'm anointed with the Spirit, I am called to serve. That's the first thing that you and I have to do in this Great Commission. If we say that Matthew 28:19-20 is for us, then we need to get rid of the religious system that has allowed some to be clergy and some to be lazy. The divisions between men and women have to be broken. The divide between sacred and secular must be broken. You're not just a businessman if you're in Christ—you're anointed and called. You are a priest just as much as someone in full-time ministry. Everybody has been called. That's what we need to embrace: the full-blown priesthood of all believers.

Secondly, we need to be sensitive to the prompting of the Spirit. This Spirit of God is a missionary Spirit. He is not only working in the church, but also in the world. In the world, He prepares the hearts of people by convicting them of their sin. They are made fertile, prepared for the seed of the gospel to germinate in their hearts. That is the work of the Holy Spirit. If you and I are priests, we need to cooperate with the Holy Spirit and be sensitive to His promptings. This will open doors into the lives of others, because the Spirit is preparing their hearts for the seed of the gospel to come from *your* mouth, your life.

Thirdly, we need prayer. We have to be working alongside God, and obeying the Great Commission. This requires prayer. Why? Because man's strategies and plans will end in failure by themselves; however, if we pray, we become more sensitive to the Holy Spirit and His strategies. This is how we walk through the open doors and share the gospel as He leads us.

In Colossians 4:2-4, Paul is talking to the church at Colossae, and he tells them, "Continue steadfastly in prayer, being watchful in it with thanksgiving. At the same time, pray also for us, that God may open to us a door for the word, to declare the mystery of Christ, on account of which I am in prison—that I may make it clear, which is how I ought to speak." When we pray, God opens doors for us to share the gospel with others! But it's important that we follow His leading.

Fourthly, we need to take that opportunity and proclaim the gospel. This good news is not for some; it's for all. It is all inclusive, for every human being. Some people may seem too far from the gospel; but the gospel is for them! Some people are from different ethnicities and different backgrounds than you; they may not fit your idea of those who are included in the gospel. Sorry, but the gospel is for all! The Jews likely thought it was difficult to share the good news to the Gentiles; but still, God breaks through and saves the Gentiles. Peter is Jewish, and he opens the gospel to the Gentiles.

Here's another thought: don't underestimate the power of homes. Your home is a powerful mission center. If you open your home and invite people who still do not know Jesus, God can use that fellowship in a powerful way. Don't underestimate the power of your home. In fact, the early church thrived and multiplied from homes to homes.

We have come to an understanding that we are priests who are to be sensitive to the promptings of the Spirit. We are to pray and be committed to sharing the good news to all. We don't leave anybody out, whether they're in the city, the country, or another nation altogether. We open up homes, because God is going to use families and living spaces. Finally, it's imperative that we partner together for the progress of the gospel. We can't do it alone. Nobody is called to do this alone. We need to partner with our local churches.

It's the church that's engaged in the city. *As a community*, we go forth with youth programs, college outreaches, night schools, and organizations. If we cooperate with the local church to make long-term differences, we'll truly impact our cities for Christ. That's what fulfilling the Great Commission looks like.

God will take you into certain places where He knows you'll be effective. God wants you to partner with the local church and the apostolic leaders. In Philippians 4:14-19, Paul expresses His gratitude for the church of Philippi and their partnership with him:

"Yet it was kind of you to share my trouble. And you Philippians yourselves know that in the beginning of the gospel, when I left Macedonia, no church entered into partnership with me in giving and receiving, except you only. Even in Thessalonica you sent me help for my needs once and again. Not that I seek the gift, but I seek the fruit that increases to your credit. I have received full payment, and more. I am well supplied, having received from Epaphroditus the gifts you sent, a fragrant offering, a sacrifice acceptable and pleasing to God. And my God will supply every need of yours according to his riches in glory in Christ Jesus."

Understand that you are called to be a priest. Don't wait for somebody else to fill your role. Be open to going wherever God calls you. This gospel is for everyone. Be sensitive to the Holy Spirit. Pray. Share. God is going use us. Amen.

EVERY TONGUE, TRIBE, AND NATION

Ed Stetzer

My name is Ed Stetzer, and I lead the Wheaton College Billy Graham Center. I'm excited to share with you now, as well as to join you in Jerusalem for Jerusalem2020. Right now, I want to talk about a church on the move—the Pentecostal influence in global Christianity, by which I'm referring to both the Pentecostal movement in its traditional form, from Azusa forward, as well as the charismatic movement that eventually moved through the mainline denominations, which was the way I came to Christ; this also encompasses what Peter Wagner called the third wave, which included churches that believed in all the gifts of the Holy Spirit, but perhaps have slightly different views about how the baptism of the Holy Spirit occurs. So I'm going to talk about the church itself, and then the influence of Pentecostalism and the Spirit-filled movement, as well.

The logical first question is, "Why is the church on the move?" It's clear that it is. For a century, the global center of Christianity was Jerusalem; then it became Rome; at times it was Constantinople. There are historical periods in which it was Russia, and then England, and then the U.S. Today, it's the global South and more—the church is definitely on the move. The church moves because Jesus says, "As the Father has sent me, so send I you." God's people responding to God's call is what puts the church on the move. Chris Wright reminds us this way: "It's not so much the case that God has a mission for his church in the world as that God has a church for his mission in the world."

God's on a mission and he's using churches around the world. It's interesting to see how the church moves. Acts 1:8 says, "You shall receive power when the Holy Spirit comes upon you, to be my witnesses in Jerusalem, Judea, Samaria, and to the uttermost parts of the earth." This makes it clear that the church was not meant to stay in Jerusalem. We sometimes do that—stay where we're comfortable; and it's not bad or sinful. But the clear command of Jesus is to go to that uttermost parts of the earth—that's where we live today. As we go through this verse, the places the disciples are called get more and more unfamiliar. Jerusalem is filled with people of the same worldview as them; Judea and Samaria, while more diverse, still had some connection in their worldviews and cultures. However, the uttermost parts of the earth represent a remarkably different worldview.

This is the movement of the church. We know that Jesus says the good news—the kingdom—will be preached throughout the whole world. All the nations will hear it, and then the end will come. We don't know exactly how that works, but we know that there's a clear calling in Matthew 24:14: that the whole world will know.

Why does this matter? Well, let's return to the question, How is the church to move? The early church proclaimed the gospel, and brought about a break from Judaism. Paul and others take missionary journeys, which see converts in Europe and beyond. But then, there's persecution, suffering and church planting. These phases lead to a global movement of which we are all a part. Rodney Stark in his book, *Cities of God*, talks about how Christianity became an urban religion and eventually conquered the Roman empire.

What we know is the church grows in the first century, but not maybe as people expected. In the second and third centuries, there are plagues, and the Christians care for the poor and the sick. The gospel is proclaimed. One emperor, Julian the apostate, would eventually complain that he tried to bring back paganism and he couldn't, because the Christians kept caring for people and sharing the gospel. By the time we get to the year 313, there's the Edict of Milan. By the time we get to 380, Christianity is actually the official religion of an empire. Christianity is always on the move.

Over and over again, we see this movement of the gospel and what that ultimately means for us. We look maybe to the reformation in 1517, and Martin Luther's 95 theses; we see Calvin's institutes in 1538; we jump forward to John Wesley, who is a remarkable influence—some have said the most influential evangelist since the apostle Paul. We look into the 1700s and 1800s and see more moves of God there—awakenings, revivals, and more. For a conversation in the Spirit-filled context, we've ultimately got to look at Azusa. Now we know that there's precursors to Azusa; but from 1906, that building on North Bonnie Brae street really changes everything when it comes to global Christianity It can't be underestimated what happens.

By 1910, the ecumenical movement is said to have begun a missionary conference. Then, evangelicals separate themselves and create a neo-evangelical movement in the fifties and sixties. People like Billy Graham and Carl Henry are involved in this shift, and they reach out to people like Oral Roberts. What happens is there's a connection between that Spirit-filled stream and this more traditional evangelical stream; they start to interact and intersect. This has been the story of the last few decades. The spread of Christian work, life, practice becomes very evident.

So what we have to ask is, "How are we doing, ultimately?" One of the things I mentioned is the growth in the global South. I've written a book in Brazilian Portuguese with a pastor based in Brazil. We did a research project on the church of Brazil; it's clear there will be more evangelicals in Brazil than in the U.S. in just a decade or two. We have to look at the Spirit-filled Pentecostal charismatic revival in Central and South America. That's one of the most significant movements in history. It's pretty stunning, the growth that's there. We have to look at that and say, "What does this mean for us?"

We're going to celebrate, pray together, and learn from one another in Jerusalem. I'm going to share some things in Jerusalem, because the Lord has given me a word about what the future might be for the continuation movement—how we can effectively and wisely steward it. We gather together in Jerusalem for a reason. You can't talk about Pentecostal charismatic third wave without talking about tongues, for example. It's important to remember that our gathering in Jerusalem is more than just a symbol.

The people of God in the Old Testament were on a mission too. As matter of fact, Jesus says once to the Pharisees, "You'll cross the ocean for a single convert." I mean, that's a pretty big deal; one soul matters. In the Old Testament, the mission was to go from Jerusalem to the nations and bring them up to Jerusalem. That's powerful and amazing. The mission was laid out in Isaiah; the Psalmist writes about this, as well. In lots of places in the Old Testament, they would go up to Jerusalem so that men and women from every tongue, tribe, and nation would be in Jerusalem worshiping the one, true God. And in this miraculous moment, God's Holy Spirit comes and descends like tongues of fire. What's worth noticing is that they hear their own languages. It was a prophetic moment, where God, in His grace and goodness says, "You know what you were supposed to do in the Old Testament? This is what it would have looked like in Jerusalem if you had done it."

It's also a prophetic picture of Revelation 7, where men and women from every tongue, tribe, and nation will gather around the throne, giving praise to God forever. So, there's this moment in Jerusalem—this powerful encounter when the Holy Spirit comes down, when Acts 1:8 is lived out before our eyes. It's very easy for us to forget that, once again, the church is on the move. As the church is on the move, there are things the church is called to do—to undertake. For example, just one of those things is reaching the unreached people groups of the world. Using the Joshua Project number from 2019, there, there are still 7,103 out of 17,073 total people groups who are classified as "unreached."

So there's not yet going to be men and women from every tongue, tribe, and nation around the throne, if those—what we call in missiology—ethnolinguistic people groups are not included yet. These are groups of people in which no one has the good news of Jesus—the praises of Jesus—on their lips. There's no one looking to tell them; they're unengaged and unreached. So if the church is on the move, does that mean our task is done because its growing around the world? Quite the contrary. If you're watching this, you're on a Great Commission highway: somebody told you the good news; and somebody told that person; somebody told that person…and it goes all the way back.

ABLAZE—A PROPHETIC CALL TO IGNITE THE CHURCH

For me, it was the charismatic movement of the Episcopal Church. I heard the gospel there and walked in newness of life. I learned what it means to walk in the Spirit. Somebody told me; somebody led me to Christ—a youth pastor by the name of Mark who shared the gospel with me in a youth group. Someone told Mark. What I want to say to those in the fastest-growing movement in the history of global Christianity is this: don't let your life or your movement become a cul-de-sac on the Great Commission highway. One way we end up doing that is we spend all of our time getting Presbyterians, Baptists, Lutherans to be Spirit-filled.

Instead, let's be thankful there are followers of Jesus from different traditions. Let's recognize that a whole lot of people don't know Jesus at all; we want them to be part of the great throne worship: men and women from every tongue, tribe, and nation. Let's remember that there are 41% of the world's people groups unreached. Let's remember that call, and engage that.

According to Joshua Project numbers, 10% of the world's population are Christ followers. About 22% of the world's population are those of nominal Christian adherence. That's double the active believers! But 39% have heard, but haven't responded to, the gospel; and 29% of the world's population have virtually no exposure to the gospel.

If the church is on the move, and God is using the Spirit-filled movement in powerful ways, what might we see as we look to 2020 and beyond? Wouldn't it be wonderful if, at Jerusalem, God impassioned and emboldened with a greater passion to reach these unreached people groups? To show and share the love of Jesus to a hurting world? To be bold in proclamation and loving in compassion? There's more work to be done. There are more people to be reached.

I would say that, in all likelihood, the late 20th century will be labeled as the global Pentecostal explosion. But my question, and what I'll talk more about in Jerusalem is, "What does that mean for the last and the least?" What does it mean that there are still people from different languages, tongues, tribes and nations in need of the gospel? As Pentecostalism has been blessed by God, God has obviously been working in and among the continuationist movement. He's working through other movements, as well; but clearly, God has been moving.

My encouragement and expectation for you is this: let's ask the Lord how he might honor by allowing us to be a part of the great and final work of the gospel. Jerusalem is a great picture for these things. Remember, this is where we get the picture of the Old Testament mission. As we gather together in Jerusalem for the event led by Empowered21, we'll actually be worshiping together in ways that point to that same picture. I hope we live with a greater heart for men and women who don't know Christ: people groups who need to hear the call of the gospel. And ultimately, I pray that we might hear the words of Jesus again: "The Holy Spirit will come upon you and you'll be my witnesses in Jerusalem, Judea, Samaria, and to the uttermost parts of the earth."

I look forward to seeing you at Jerusalem2020.

JERUSALEM2020 SPEAKERS

Heidi Baker is "Mama Heidi" to thousands of children, and oversees a broad holistic ministry that includes Bible schools, medical clinics, church-based orphan care, well drilling, primary schools, evangelistic and healing outreaches in remote villages and a network of thousands of churches.

Bill Johnson and his wife, Beni Johnson, serve a growing number of churches that have partnered for revival. This apostolic network has crossed denominational lines in building relationships that enable church leaders to walk in both purity and power.

Michael Koulianos is the founder of Jesus Events, which thousands attend in cities across America, and Jesus School, a ministry school focused on raising up a Jesus people who will shake the world with the love of God.

Nathan Morris travels around the world with a burning passion to preach the Gospel of Jesus Christ to all nations and to see the power of the Holy Spirit demonstrated.

Samuel Rodriguez has been identified by *The Wall Street Journal* as one of America's seven most influential Hispanic Leaders, and the only religious leader on the list.

Cindy Jacobs is a respected prophet who travels the world ministering to believers, and to heads of nations. Perhaps her greatest ministry is to world influencers who seek her prophetic advice.

ABLAZE—A PROPHETIC CALL TO IGNITE THE CHURCH

Andy Byrd and his wife Holly have dedicated their lives to spiritual awakening in a generation. Andy is part of the leadership of University of the Nations, YWAM Kona and has been with YWAM for 19 years.

César Castellanos and his wife, Claudia Castellanos, have pastored International Charismatic Mission (MCI), one of the fastest growing churches in Latin America, for more than 30 years.

Paul Dhinakaran and his ministry have led millions in experiencing divine peace and well-being. Broken families have been rebuilt and have found a new meaning in life.

Russell Evans serves as senior pastor of Planetshakers Church, which was launched in Melbourne, Australia in 2004. To date, every service has included a salvation altar call resulting in over 25,000 first-time decisions and still counting!

Todd Johnson is a professor of global Christianity and director of the Center for the Study of Global Christianity at Gordon-Conwell Theological Seminary.

Jean-Luc Trachsel works actively to bring unity among Christians and to proclaim the gospel with mercy and compassion to this generation.

Kenneth Ulmer is the former president of The King's College and Seminary, where he is also a founding board member and adjunct professor.

Ed Stetzer holds the recently-created Billy Graham Distinguished Chair for Church, Mission, and Evangelism at Wheaton College, and also serves as the Executive Director of the Billy Graham Center.

Robert Hoskins took leadership of OneHope in 2004, and since has continued to advance the vision of God's Word. Under Rob's leadership, OneHope has worked in over 179 countries and translated their programs into hundreds of languages.

Niko Njotorahardjo started a congregation in Jakarta in 1988 with 400 persons and now the church has exceeded 250,000 members, with 6,000 cell groups and 900 branches in Indonesia and around the world.

Stovall Weems is the founder and senior pastor of Celebration Church in Jacksonville, Florida. Since 1998, Celebration has grown to 12,000 in weekly attendance and now includes local, regional, and international campuses.

Goodwill Shana is the founder and senior pastor of Word of Life International Ministries founded in the City of Bulawayo, Zimbabwe in 1990. Starting with a congregation of four, the church has grown to over 15,000 members in five branches across the world including Zimbabwe, South Africa, Botswana, Lesotho, Australia, and the United Kingdom.

Billy Wilson currently serves as the fourth president of Oral Roberts University. He is the host of a weekly television program, World Impact with Billy Wilson, which is seen in over 170 nations. Dr. Wilson has also fostered unique global partnerships through Empowered21.

George Wood served as General Superintendent of the General Council of the Assemblies of God in the United States of America (AG) from 2007-2017 and has been Chairman of the World Assemblies of God Fellowship, the largest Pentecostal denomination in the world, since 2008.

ABLAZE—A PROPHETIC CALL TO IGNITE THE CHURCH

Chadwick Mohan is the lead pastor of New Life Assembly of God Church in Chennai, India. Chad is deeply committed to establishing the Church as a family of families, which is relationally mentored through every stage of life and lived as the family of God in small groups.

Jentezen Franklin is the senior pastor of Free Chapel, a multi-campus church. Each week, his television program, Kingdom Connection, is broadcast on major networks all over the world. A *New York Times* best-selling author, Jentezen has written nine books, including his most recent, *Love Like You've Never Been Hurt*, the groundbreaking *Fasting*, and *Right People-Right Place-Right Plan*.

JERUSALEM2020 CONFERENCE NOTES

JERUSALEM2020 CONFERENCE NOTES

www.ingramcontent.com/pod-product-compliance
Lightning Source LLC
Chambersburg PA
CBHW022108090426
42743CB00008B/764